SPECTRUMS UNSEEN

A Journey Through Hidden Worlds

(Monochrome Edition)

Knox

Disclaimer

The ideas, concepts, and speculations presented in this book, *Spectrums Unseen*, are intended for educational and philosophical exploration. This work is a creative reflection on the nature of perception, reality, and the possible existence of parallel worlds, and is not intended to assert factual claims about the existence of larger forces, cosmic beings, or unseen realities.

The discussions within this book are based on interpretations of scientific, philosophical, and speculative frameworks. Readers are encouraged to explore these concepts with an open mind while recognizing that they remain within the realm of theory and imagination.

The author does not claim expertise in any specific scientific or philosophical discipline, and the content should not be taken as definitive conclusions or advice on matters of science, religion, or cosmology. The reader's own critical thinking and personal interpretation are encouraged in engaging with the material.

Any resemblance to actual persons, living or dead, events, or entities is purely coincidental.

Preface

In our daily lives, we exist at a crossroads of the seen and unseen, where the tangible meets the intangible, and the known intertwines with the mysterious. *Spectrums Unseen* is born from a curiosity that seeks to explore these hidden realms — the dimensions of existence that elude our perception but profoundly shape our reality. Each chapter delves into the vast, intricate web that connects all forms of life, matter, and energy, inviting readers on a journey through worlds within and beyond the visible.

This book is a reflection of humanity's timeless desire to understand the unknown. It draws inspiration from the endless frontiers of science, philosophy, and the natural world. Through exploring the layers of reality that lie beyond our senses, *Spectrums Unseen* aims to awaken a sense of wonder, inviting readers to ponder the vast and complex nature of existence. It is a journey into a universe that is larger, more intricate, and more interconnected than we might ever fully grasp — a reminder that there is always more to discover, and always more to see. Thank you for joining me on this journey of discovery.

— **Knox**

Introduction

Our world is shaped by the limits of our perception, confined by the edges of what we can see, hear, and touch. Yet, just beyond these boundaries lies a vast and invisible universe teeming with forces and phenomena that quietly govern our reality. As human beings, we are naturally inclined to seek answers, to illuminate the dark corners of the unknown, and to stretch the boundaries of our understanding.

In *Spectrums Unseen*, we embark on a journey to explore these hidden dimensions, examining the cosmic, the microscopic, and the theoretical in pursuit of a deeper understanding of the universe and our place within it. From the dark matter that holds galaxies together to the fractal patterns that underlie the structure of nature, from the microbial ecosystems within our bodies to the possible existence of multiple dimensions, this book aims to reveal the invisible architectures that shape our world.

As we navigate these uncharted territories, we find that our reality is built upon layers of complexity, where each layer offers a glimpse into the interconnectedness of all things. We discover that the universe is not only more immense than we imagine, but also more wondrously connected — a tapestry of visible and invisible threads, woven together in a dance that extends beyond our senses.

Join me as we journey into the unseen, into the spaces where science, philosophy, and imagination converge.

Together, we will explore a universe that is as mysterious as it is beautiful, and we will question the nature of reality, perception, and the possibilities that lie beyond.

Table of Contents

Chapter 1: The Microscopic Frontier: Bacteria's World of Survival

"A single drop of water can be an entire universe for the smallest life forms. To them, the vast world we know is invisible, their existence intertwined with forces they can never comprehend."

In the boundless tapestry of life, there exist creatures so small they often escape our notice: bacteria. These single-celled organisms inhabit a universe vastly different from our own, where their homes can be as small as a grain of soil, the surface of a leaf, or the folds of our skin. A world that might be imperceptible to us is, for them, teeming with mountains, oceans, and fields— spaces they explore with relentless persistence.

Imagine yourself shrinking down to their size, suddenly cast into a droplet of water where every ripple feels like a tidal wave, and every grain of sand is a boulder to navigate. Here, bacteria flourish, isolated from the human-scale world, where distances are measured in microns and the stakes are high, with every moment a race for survival. In this chapter, we'll dive into their world, uncovering the intricacies of their existence and how their struggle for life reminds us of the power—and limitations—of perception.

A World Measured in Microns

In the bacterial realm, proximity is everything. The distance we casually cover with a single step is, for them, an odyssey. A few microns—a millionth of a meter—might separate a bacterium from a food source, but in their world, it is as significant as a day's journey. Bacteria navigate their surroundings using **chemotaxis**, a fascinating process where they detect chemical gradients and respond accordingly. Think of it as their internal GPS, directing them toward nutrients and away from danger.

Picture a bacterium drifting in a droplet of water. To our eyes, this is an invisible speck, but to the bacterium, it is an entire ocean, bustling with resources, competitors, and predators. Here, it drifts, using minuscule, hair-like structures called **flagella** to propel itself forward. As it twists and tumbles, it encounters an invisible plume of nutrients and is drawn towards it, like a sailor spotting land after days at sea. It knows nothing of the human face it resides on, nor of the air currents above. Its reality is confined to this microcosm, where every micron counts.

Rapid Evolution: Survival of the Fittest

While we humans may take decades to witness noticeable changes in our species, bacteria live in fast-forward. A single bacterium can reproduce multiple times within an hour, passing on genetic material to new generations with lightning speed. This rapid reproduction fuels their evolution, allowing bacteria to adapt quickly to new challenges, whether it's a change in temperature, the arrival of a new competitor, or the presence of antibiotics.

Some bacteria, like *Deinococcus radiodurans*, are famously resilient. Known as the "Conan the Bacterium," it can survive doses of radiation that would obliterate a human, endure extreme drought, and even repair its own DNA after massive damage. Such capabilities have enabled bacteria to not only survive but thrive in environments as hostile as radioactive waste sites and the acidic hot springs of Yellowstone. They've even hitched rides on spacecraft, enduring the harsh vacuum of space, seemingly ready to colonize any world they encounter.

But with this rapid evolution comes a downside for us. In our battle against bacterial infections, antibiotics play a crucial role, yet bacteria have developed an unsettling knack for resistance. When exposed to antibiotics, some bacteria can swap genes with one another, sharing resistance traits like secrets passed in the dark. In a matter of weeks, an entire population can become immune to drugs that once held them at bay. For humans, it's a daunting reminder of how quickly bacteria adapt, evolving to survive against even our most potent defences.

Bacteria and the Human Body: An Invisible Partnership

Although bacteria often get a bad reputation as agents of disease, they are also our allies, existing in a delicate symbiosis with us. The human body is host to trillions of bacteria, collectively known as the **human microbiome**. These microscopic companions live on our skin, in our mouths, and within our digestive system, where they play an indispensable role in maintaining our health.

Consider the gut, home to a diverse community of bacteria that help break down food, produce essential vitamins, and even regulate our immune system. Without these tiny helpers, our bodies would struggle to digest certain foods and fend off harmful pathogens. They communicate with our cells, sending chemical signals that influence everything from digestion to mood, shaping our well-being in ways we are only beginning to understand.

Yet, as essential as they are, bacteria remain blissfully unaware of the larger world they inhabit. They know nothing of human thoughts or emotions. They drift through their microscopic domain, where we are nothing more than an intricate landscape, a world that feeds and shelters them but remains as mysterious to them as the cosmos is to us.

The Invisible Forces Shaping Bacterial Life

Bacteria operate within a framework of invisible forces, just as we do. While they may not comprehend them, these forces shape their lives in profound ways. Temperature shifts, moisture changes, and antibiotic encounters can alter their environment dramatically, forcing them to adapt or face extinction. These forces are as inexplicable to them as cosmic forces like dark matter and gravity are to us.

For instance, when exposed to a sudden burst of heat, some bacteria initiate a process called **sporulation,** where they encase themselves in a tough shell to withstand extreme conditions. This adaptation, much like a human taking shelter from a storm, allows them to survive until favourable conditions return. To them, these environmental changes are no more understandable than the concept of a universe expanding into infinity is to us. They simply react, their lives governed by forces beyond their comprehension.

A Reflection on Scale

The world of bacteria serves as a reminder that perception is always bound by scale. To them, reality is confined to the microscopic, where survival is a matter of milliseconds and microns. They live in a world of chemical gradients and instinctual responses, completely unaware of the larger forces that shape their existence. In turn, we, too, are bound by our human-scale perception, often oblivious to the vast cosmic forces that govern the universe.

Yet bacteria, in their obliviousness, play vital roles in ecosystems, from aiding in nutrient cycling to helping us digest food. Though they cannot comprehend the larger systems they support, their existence is essential to life as we know it. Similarly, we inhabit a universe filled with invisible forces—gravity, electromagnetism, and possibly dark matter—that influence our lives in ways we may never fully grasp.

In the end, the world of bacteria challenges us to consider our own limitations. Like them, we exist in a reality layered with complexity, where much remains beyond our perception. But by peering into their microscopic universe, we gain insights into the interconnectedness of all life, a reminder that we are part of something far more intricate and profound than we may ever fully understand.

"A bacterium will never see the world as we do. In their tiny universe, the vast forces we take for granted remain unknown. Yet, they persist—small but essential, each an individual part of the larger web of life."

Chapter 2: The Ant's Universe: Navigating a Towering World

"To an ant, a blade of grass is a towering tree, a single step can be a great journey, and the world is defined by the forces it cannot understand but instinctively navigates."

In the dense undergrowth of forests, gardens, and fields, millions of tiny creatures live their lives in a world that, from their perspective, is vast and towering. Among these are ants, social insects that have thrived on Earth for over 100 million years. Ants have an extraordinary ability to cooperate, forming colonies that function almost like a single, unified organism. But how does an ant experience this complex world? How does it navigate an environment where every aspect, from a drop of water to a blade of grass, looms large?

From an ant's perspective, its environment is an immense landscape of endless challenges and opportunities. A single blade of grass could be a skyscraper, and a pebble could be a mountain. The ground under our feet is, to them, an intricate tapestry of scents, textures, and hidden trails. By delving into their perception, we can gain insights into how they navigate this towering world and how their survival is intricately linked to their unique way of seeing things.

The World Through Ant Senses

While humans primarily rely on sight and sound, ants live in a world dominated by **chemical signals**. Ants use their highly sensitive antennae to detect **pheromones**, which are chemical messages that guide their behaviour, alert them to danger, and direct them to food. For ants, these chemical trails are like invisible highways, allowing them to navigate their environment with remarkable precision.

Imagine yourself as an ant, venturing out from the nest for the first time. To human eyes, your journey may look random, but it is anything but. You are following a carefully laid path of pheromones, each step taking you closer to a source of food or back to the safety of the colony. As you make your way, you touch the ground with your antennae, reading the chemical signals left by other ants, sensing a faint sweetness that grows stronger as you get closer to a food source.

Ants also have **compound eyes**, which can detect movement and light but lack the ability to form detailed images. Instead, ants "see" their world through touch and smell, with each antenna acting as a finely tuned instrument that picks up a wealth of information. Their perception is not shaped by visual landmarks as ours is but by chemical cues that convey all they need to know. This way of sensing the world is so different from ours that it is almost unimaginable; for ants, a world without pheromones would be as disorienting as a world without light is to us.

The Colony: A Superorganism at Work

Ant colonies are not just collections of individuals but complex systems that function like **superorganisms**. Each ant has a role—some forage for food, others care for the young, while soldiers protect the nest. The queen, though often seen as the leader, is more accurately described as the reproductive center of the colony, laying thousands of eggs but not directing the actions of the workers. Instead, ants communicate and coordinate through simple rules and chemical signals, with no need for a central command.

Consider the leafcutter ants of the Amazon rainforest. These ants are farmers, cutting leaves from plants and carrying them back to their underground nests. But they don't eat the leaves; instead, they use them to cultivate a special type of fungus, which serves as their primary food source. Each ant follows a set of basic instructions, but together, they achieve an incredible feat of agriculture. Leafcutter ants can strip entire trees of their leaves, yet they avoid killing the plants, maintaining a delicate balance with their environment.

This division of labour and the ants' ability to work as a collective allows the colony to adapt and thrive in changing conditions. Ants don't need a leader because their collective intelligence emerges from individual actions, a phenomenon that has inspired algorithms in computer science and robotics. Swarm intelligence, as it is known, demonstrates how simple behaviours, when repeated across a group, can result in highly organized and efficient solutions to complex problems.

Navigating a Giant World

To an ant, navigating the world is a monumental task. Every step covers a vast distance, and every obstacle poses a challenge. Ants face dangers we might overlook—raindrops that are like boulders falling from the sky, gusts of wind that could send them tumbling, and shadows that bring sudden darkness. Despite these challenges, ants navigate their environment with incredible skill, using a combination of **landmark-based navigation** and **internal compasses**.

Ants are known to use the position of the sun to orient themselves. By keeping track of the angle of the sun relative to their position, they can maintain a sense of direction even after long journeys. Desert ants, for instance, can travel hundreds of meters across the sand to find food and then return to their nests with astonishing accuracy. They do this by calculating the angle of the sun and using polarized light patterns in the sky, which they can detect through specialized cells in their eyes.

Beyond natural landmarks, ants also rely on their internal sense of time, counting their steps as they move. This combination of spatial awareness and temporal tracking allows them to navigate a world that seems immense to them, finding their way through an intricate network of chemical trails and environmental cues. It is a testament to their adaptability that ants can navigate such a vast world with their simple, yet highly effective, sensory tools.

The Ant's Perception of Humans: Giants in the Landscape

To an ant, humans are like mythical giants—colossal, unpredictable forces that occasionally disrupt their world. When we pass through their environment, ants don't perceive us as individuals but rather as forces of nature, akin to storms or floods. A footstep near an ant colony might send vibrations through the ground, triggering alarm signals that spread through the colony like wildfire.

In the face of human disruption, ants respond with instinctive resilience. If a section of the colony is destroyed, ants will quickly begin to rebuild, showing no signs of fear or anger. They simply act, following the pheromone cues that drive them to repair their home. They cannot comprehend our thoughts or emotions; to them, we are part of the landscape, immense and unknowable.

This relationship between ants and humans reflects our own relationship with the cosmos. Just as ants cannot understand the beings that alter their environment, we struggle to grasp the cosmic forces that shape our lives. Gravity, dark matter, and other fundamental forces are to us what human footsteps are to ants—ever-present, powerful, and largely beyond our understanding.

The Power of Collective Intelligence

Ants exhibit a remarkable form of intelligence known as **swarm intelligence**, where individuals follow simple rules, yet their collective behaviour results in sophisticated problem-solving. For example, when ants encounter a flooded path, they will begin to build bridges with their own bodies, forming living structures that allow others to cross. This behaviour isn't directed by any single ant but emerges spontaneously from the colony as a whole.

In this way, ants demonstrate that intelligence does not have to be centralized. Through basic rules and interactions, they achieve feats of coordination that rival those of larger, more complex organisms. This decentralized intelligence has inspired human technologies, such as drone swarms and optimization algorithms, showing that ants, despite their size, can teach us valuable lessons about adaptability and cooperation.

One fascinating example of swarm intelligence is found in **army ants**, which form massive raiding columns that sweep through forests, capturing prey in their path. These columns can stretch for hundreds of meters and contain thousands of ants, all moving in unison. They flow around obstacles, split into smaller groups to pursue different prey, and then rejoint, all without any central direction. It is as if the colony itself is alive, a single organism made up of countless individuals.

Conclusion: A Giant World in Miniature

To an ant, the world is immense, filled with towering structures and vast distances. Their lives are shaped by the chemical signals they follow, the needs of their colony, and their instinctual responses to the environment. Despite their small size, ants have developed complex strategies for survival, cooperation, and navigation, all while remaining blissfully unaware of the larger forces at play.

The ant's universe reminds us that perception is relative. For ants, humans are incomprehensible giants, part of an unpredictable landscape that occasionally reshapes their lives. As we ponder the mysteries of existence, from the smallest cells to the largest galaxies, we should remember that our perception of reality is just one of many possible ways to experience the world. The universe, like the world of ants, is far more complex and interconnected than we may ever realize.

"To an ant, a blade of grass is a towering tree, a single step can be a great journey, and the world is defined by the forces it cannot understand but instinctively navigate."

Chapter 3: The Human Scale: A World of Observation

"We stand at the middle of a vast scale—from the microscopic to the cosmic. Our world feels expansive, full of meaning and understanding, yet our perception is confined to what our senses and tools allow us to grasp."

At the human scale, we occupy a unique position in the universe. We are neither as minuscule as bacteria, nor as colossal as stars. Our size grants us a sense of mastery over our surroundings—we observe, interact with, and reshape the world according to our will. Yet, despite this, our perception is limited. How much of the universe do we truly understand, and how much remains hidden, just beyond the reach of our senses?

Human experience is profoundly shaped by the sensory tools we possess. Our eyes reveal only a sliver of the electromagnetic spectrum, our ears capture a narrow band of sound frequencies, and our sense of touch connects us only to surfaces we can reach. Though our senses offer us a vivid experience of reality, they also restrict us to a small fraction of what truly exists. In this chapter, we will explore the boundaries of human perception, examining how we observe the world and how our tools extend—but also constrain—our understanding of the cosmos.

The Window of Human Perception

Sight is perhaps our most dominant sense, colouring our perception of the world with light and shadow. However, what we see—the **visible spectrum**—represents only a tiny fraction of the electromagnetic spectrum. The colours we perceive are limited to wavelengths between approximately 400 and 700 nanometres. Beyond these limits lie entire realms of radiation that we cannot detect without assistance.

Imagine the world through infrared eyes, where heat radiates visibly from every object. Trees, animals, and even the ground itself would emit a soft glow, revealing patterns of warmth invisible to our natural vision. Or consider the ultraviolet spectrum, which influences ecosystems in ways we cannot perceive. Bees, for instance, can see ultraviolet light, allowing them to spot patterns on flowers that guide them to nectar. To a bee, flowers may appear as vibrant roadmaps, while to us, they are simply colourful blooms.

Similarly, our perception of sound is confined to a narrow frequency range, typically between 20 and 20,000 Hertz. Animals like dolphins and bats operate in a world of **ultrasonic frequencies**, using echolocation to navigate and hunt. They emit high-pitched sounds that bounce off objects, returning echoes that map out their surroundings with precision. To them, sound paints a picture of the world as vivid as the one we see with our eyes, yet completely alien to us.

These sensory limitations shape our understanding of reality. We perceive only a thin slice of the spectrum of existence, unaware of the myriad phenomena occurring beyond our reach. The electromagnetic and auditory landscapes that surround us are largely invisible, and without the aid of technology, we would remain oblivious to their presence.

The Illusion of Comprehension

Though we rely on our senses to navigate the world, they offer us only a partial representation of reality. When we gaze at the night sky, we see only pinpoints of starlight, scattered across a dark canvas. However, stars emit a range of radiation, including X-rays and gamma rays, which we cannot detect with our eyes. It is only through telescopes and other instruments that we uncover the hidden aspects of the universe, revealing celestial bodies and cosmic phenomena that lie far beyond the reach of human vision.

Yet, even with advanced technology, our understanding is far from complete. The images we see from telescopes are often manipulated, translated into colours and forms we can comprehend. In a sense, our perception of the cosmos remains tethered to our human scale, mediated by instruments that extend our senses but do not transform them. We are limited to interpreting these signals in ways that make sense to our minds, a process that can both enlighten and deceive.

This illusion of comprehension gives us a sense of control, a belief that we grasp the forces shaping our universe. Yet, what we truly understand is only a fraction of the whole. The vastness of the cosmos and the intricacy of quantum realms hint at a deeper reality that lies beyond our perceptual grasp, an underlying structure that may never be fully revealed.

The Human Experience of Time

In addition to our sensory limitations, our perception of time is deeply subjective. Time shapes everything from the orbits of planets to the lifespans of living beings, yet our experience of it is bound by our biological rhythms and emotional states. A single day can feel long or short, depending on how we spend it, but in the context of the universe, it is barely a blink.

We measure time in seconds, minutes, and years, creating a linear narrative that helps us make sense of our lives. However, time itself is not fixed—it bends and warps under extreme conditions, as Einstein's theory of relativity reveals. Near a black hole, for instance, time slows dramatically due to intense gravitational forces, while in the quantum realm, particles can exist in states that defy our conventional understanding of past, present, and future.

Our perception of time is also limited by the scales at which we live. While we experience life in decades, stars live for billions of years, and tectonic shifts that reshape continents unfold over eons. Just as bacteria perceive time differently due to their rapid life cycles, we too are limited by our own temporal framework. In the grand tapestry of cosmic time, our lives are brief, and our understanding of time's true nature remains elusive.

Tools of Perception: Extending Our Reach

Despite our sensory limitations, humans have developed tools that allow us to glimpse beyond the boundaries of our natural perception. **Telescopes** bring distant galaxies into view, while **microscopes** reveal the intricate world of cells and microorganisms. These instruments extend our senses, allowing us to explore realms that would otherwise be inaccessible.

Consider the Hubble Space Telescope, which has provided us with breathtaking images of nebulae, star clusters, and galaxies billions of light-years away. Through its lens, we see the birth and death of stars, the swirling arms of galaxies, and the faint glow of cosmic phenomena that occurred long before Earth existed. Or think about the Large Hadron Collider, a machine that smashes particles together at near-light speeds to reveal the fundamental building blocks of matter. These tools push the boundaries of our understanding, yet they also remind us of how much remains unknown.

Even with these advancements, our perception of reality is incomplete. For every answer we uncover, new questions arise, hinting at hidden dimensions and forces we have yet to understand. Dark matter and dark energy, for example, make up most of the universe's mass and energy, yet they remain undetectable except through their gravitational effects. These invisible forces suggest that there is far more to the universe than meets the eye, and our current tools may only scratch the surface of a far deeper mystery.

A World of Invisible Forces

The universe is filled with forces that shape our reality, yet most are invisible to our senses. **Gravity** holds planets in orbit, binds galaxies together, and keeps us grounded, yet we cannot see it directly. Instead, we perceive its effects—the fall of an apple, the trajectory of a thrown ball, the weight that presses us against the Earth.

Magnetic fields guide the migration of animals and protect our planet from harmful solar radiation. Without them, Earth would be vulnerable to cosmic rays, stripping away our atmosphere and rendering life impossible. Yet, these fields remain invisible to us, detectable only through their influence on charged particles and their effects on the compasses we use for navigation.

Beyond these familiar forces lie even more mysterious phenomena, like **dark matter** and **dark energy**, which make up about 95% of the universe. Though we cannot observe them directly, their presence is inferred from the way galaxies move and the way the universe expands. These forces challenge our understanding of reality, reminding us that what we perceive is only a sliver of what truly exists.

Conclusion: The Middle Ground of Perception

Humans exist at the midpoint between the microscopic and the cosmic, occupying a narrow band of reality shaped by the limitations of our senses. Our tools allow us to glimpse beyond these boundaries, revealing wonders that lie beyond human perception. Yet, for all our advancements, we remain creatures of the human scale, tethered to our own subjective experience of time and space.

As we explore the universe, we are constantly reminded of the vastness that lies beyond our grasp. The human scale provides us with a unique perspective, but it is only one of countless ways to perceive the world. As we continue to extend our reach, uncovering new mysteries and unlocking new dimensions of understanding, we must remember that our perception is but a narrow window into a far greater reality.

"We stand at the middle of a vast scale—from the microscopic to the cosmic. Our world feels expansive, full of meaning and understanding, yet our perception is confined to what our senses and tools allow us to grasp."

Chapter 4: Unseen Forces: The Invisible Architecture of Reality

"Not everything that shapes our world can be seen. Some forces—though invisible to the naked eye—govern the very structure of reality, bending space and time, holding galaxies together, and moving through dimensions beyond our perception."

In the physical world, we are surrounded by forces that we cannot see or touch, yet they shape every aspect of our existence. Gravity holds us to the Earth, magnetism influences the behaviour of charged particles, and the electromagnetic spectrum provides the framework for light, heat, and countless other phenomena. These unseen forces create an invisible architecture, forming the very foundation upon which reality is built. We rely on them for our daily existence, but we often take them for granted, barely acknowledging their presence.

What if these forces are just the beginning? What if they offer only a glimpse into an even more complex reality, one that extends beyond our senses and even our most advanced technology? Could there be forces and dimensions that remain forever hidden from us, guiding the universe in ways we can only theorize? As we explore these unseen forces, we begin to see how they might connect us to a multidimensional universe, hinting at hidden layers of existence that shape the cosmos from behind a veil of perception.

Gravity: The Force that Binds the Universe

Gravity is perhaps the most familiar of the unseen forces, yet it remains one of the most mysterious. We experience its effects constantly; from the way objects fall to the ground to the way planets orbit the sun. According to **Einstein's theory of general relativity**, gravity is not a force in the traditional sense but rather a curvature in the fabric of spacetime. Massive objects like stars and planets bend spacetime around them, creating what we perceive as gravitational pull.

Imagine placing a heavy ball on a stretched rubber sheet. The ball creates a depression, causing smaller objects to roll towards it. This is a simplified version of how gravity works, with massive objects warping the fabric of spacetime and guiding the motion of other objects within their vicinity. This unseen curvature governs the structure of galaxies, influences the flow of time, and even affects the path of light itself, bending it around massive bodies in an effect known as **gravitational lensing**.

Yet gravity also presents us with profound mysteries. It is incredibly weak compared to the other fundamental forces—electromagnetism, the strong nuclear force, and the weak nuclear force. This weakness has puzzled scientists for decades, leading to theories that gravity might extend into **extra dimensions** beyond the three spatial dimensions we experience. According to some models in **string theory**, gravity could be "leaking" into these hidden dimensions, which would explain why it appears so much weaker in our three-dimensional world. This idea opens up tantalizing possibilities: if gravity truly exists beyond our perceived dimensions, then perhaps our universe is just one layer within a vast, multidimensional reality.

Magnetism: The Hidden Force that Shapes Our World

While gravity operates on a cosmic scale, magnetism plays a more immediate, yet equally profound, role in our lives. **Magnetic fields** influence the behaviour of charged particles, shape the Earth's environment, and even affect biological organisms. The magnetic field that surrounds Earth, generated by the movement of molten iron within its core, acts as a protective shield, deflecting harmful solar radiation and preventing it from stripping away our atmosphere. Without this invisible barrier, life as we know it would be impossible.

Magnetism also extends its reach into the animal kingdom, where it influences the behaviour of various species. Many migratory birds, for example, have specialized cells containing magnetite, a magnetic mineral that allows them to sense the Earth's magnetic field. This sense, known as **magnetoreception**, helps them navigate thousands of miles during migration, guiding them across vast distances with precision. In a similar vein, sea turtles and even some bacteria use the Earth's magnetic field to orient themselves, following unseen paths that lead them to food, breeding grounds, or safer habitats.

Like gravity, magnetism is also tied to higher-dimensional theories in physics. Some grand unified theories propose that all forces, including electromagnetism, are manifestations of a single, underlying force that fully reveals itself only in higher dimensions. If this is true, then the magnetism we experience might be a mere shadow of a deeper, more complex reality—an indication that our universe is woven from forces that extend beyond our perception.

The Electromagnetic Spectrum: Forces We Cannot See

The **electromagnetic spectrum** is an essential, yet mostly invisible, aspect of our reality. It includes not only visible light but also radio waves, microwaves, infrared, ultraviolet, X-rays, and gamma rays. Each type of electromagnetic radiation has its own unique properties and plays a role in shaping the universe, from the transmission of radio signals across vast distances to the high-energy phenomena within black holes.

Although we are surrounded by electromagnetic radiation, we can see only a tiny portion of it—what we know as **visible light**. Beyond the reds, greens, and blues of the visible spectrum lies a vast landscape of radiation that we remain unaware of without the aid of technology. **Infrared radiation** reveals the warmth of objects, allowing us to see heat. **Ultraviolet light**, while invisible to our eyes, influences ecosystems and contributes to the development of life. At the higher-energy end of the spectrum, **X-rays** and **gamma rays** expose the violent processes within stars and galaxies, hinting at cosmic events that are far beyond our everyday experience.

The electromagnetic spectrum shows us that much of the universe is hidden from view. We are blind to most of the radiation that surrounds us, relying on instruments to reveal its presence. Just as we cannot perceive most of the electromagnetic spectrum, there may be other forces and dimensions that we are equally blind to—realities that shape our existence in ways we can only begin to imagine.

The Role of Dark Matter: Invisible but Powerful

One of the greatest enigmas in modern astrophysics is **dark matter**, a mysterious substance that neither emits nor reflects light, rendering it invisible to all forms of electromagnetic detection. Despite this, dark matter is believed to make up about 85% of the matter in the universe, and its presence is inferred from its gravitational effects on galaxies and galaxy clusters. Without dark matter, these structures would not have enough mass to hold themselves together, and the universe would look vastly different.

Unlike ordinary matter, dark matter does not interact with the electromagnetic spectrum, meaning it neither absorbs, emits, nor reflects light. It passes through normal matter almost undetected, like a ghostly presence that moves silently through the cosmos. Its elusiveness has led to theories that dark matter might exist in or interact with higher dimensions, giving rise to the idea that it could be a shadow of some higher-dimensional matter.

Some physicists have even proposed that dark matter might interact with itself in ways that we cannot detect, potentially forming entire ecosystems of dark matter galaxies, stars, and planets. These "dark worlds" could exist parallel to our own, exerting gravitational influence yet remaining invisible. If dark matter truly operates in dimensions beyond our perception, it could provide clues to the nature of a **multidimensional universe**, one where our reality is but a single thread in a much larger cosmic tapestry.

Invisible Forces and Multidimensional Realities

The unseen forces that shape our reality—gravity, magnetism, and the electromagnetic spectrum—hint at the existence of hidden dimensions and realms beyond our reach. These forces suggest that the universe is far more complex and layered than it appears, perhaps stretching into realities that we cannot experience directly. In the realm of **string theory**, scientists propose that all particles and forces are vibrations of tiny, one-dimensional "strings" that exist in multiple dimensions. If these theories hold true, then our three-dimensional perception is only one aspect of a vast, interconnected reality.

The idea of **multidimensional realities** opens up intriguing possibilities. Could there be worlds beyond our own, layered upon each other like pages in a book? Might there be beings or phenomena existing in these hidden dimensions, influencing our reality in ways we cannot detect? As science advances, we edge closer to uncovering the secrets of these unseen forces, but each discovery reveals only more mysteries, pushing us to question the very nature of existence.

Conclusion: The Unseen Architecture of the Universe

We live in a world governed by forces we cannot see, yet they shape every aspect of our lives. Gravity, magnetism, and the electromagnetic spectrum create an invisible architecture that underlies our reality, while dark matter and higher dimensions suggest that there is far more to the universe than we can perceive. These unseen forces challenge our understanding of existence, reminding us that what we experience is only a tiny fraction of the whole.

As we continue to explore the boundaries of human knowledge, we are reminded of the limitations of our perception. The universe is not just vast in size but also in depth, filled with layers of reality that we are only beginning to uncover. Perhaps one day, we will unlock the secrets of these hidden forces and dimensions, revealing a universe far stranger and more intricate than we can currently imagine.

"Not everything that shapes our world can be seen. Some forces—though invisible to the naked eye—govern the very structure of reality, bending space and time, holding galaxies together, and moving through dimensions beyond our perception."

Chapter 5: Sensing Survival: Perception and Adaptation Across Scales

"Survival is shaped not just by the world we live in, but by how we perceive it. From the deepest ocean trenches to the highest mountain peaks, life adapts, and with it, perception evolves to meet the demands of each environment."

Life on Earth thrives in environments that range from the most extreme heat to the coldest depths. To survive, creatures have developed an astonishing variety of adaptations, many of which rely on unique sensory perceptions. How an organism senses its surroundings determines its ability to find food, escape predators, and navigate its world. The vast diversity of environments on our planet has led to an equally vast array of sensory adaptations, each finely tuned to meet the demands of its habitat.

In this chapter, we explore the sensory strategies of life across different scales, from creatures of the abyssal ocean depths to birds that soar at high altitudes. Each of these environments presents unique challenges, requiring specialized adaptations that reflect the remarkable diversity of perception in the natural world. These examples reveal how life shapes—and is shaped by—the way it perceives its surroundings.

The Deep Sea: A World of Darkness and Pressure

The **deep ocean** is one of the most inhospitable environments on Earth. At depths of several thousand meters, sunlight cannot penetrate, leaving the ocean floor in perpetual darkness. Temperatures hover just above freezing, and the immense water pressure would crush most surface-dwelling organisms. Yet, despite these challenges, life thrives in this abyssal realm, equipped with adaptations that allow creatures to survive in complete darkness.

Among the inhabitants of this world is the **anglerfish**, a predator with a bioluminescent lure that dangles in front of its mouth. This glowing appendage, powered by symbiotic bacteria, attracts unsuspecting prey in the darkness. The anglerfish's lure functions like a personal flashlight, illuminating the surrounding water just enough to reveal nearby prey without giving away the anglerfish's presence.

Another deep-sea marvel is the **giant squid**, which has eyes as large as dinner plates. These eyes are adapted to detect the faintest glimmers of light, such as the bioluminescence produced by other creatures. In the dark, crushing depths, this heightened sensitivity is essential for spotting both prey and predators. Meanwhile, the **gulper eel** has a highly sensitive lateral line—a row of specialized cells along its body that detect subtle changes in water pressure. This sense allows it to "feel" the presence of nearby organisms, even in complete darkness, giving it a way to navigate a world where sight is of little use.

These creatures demonstrate that even in environments where traditional senses like vision are limited, life finds a way to perceive the world. By adapting to the unique conditions of the deep sea, they reveal how survival can be linked to the evolution of specialized sensory abilities that go beyond our human experience.

Deserts: Heat, Scarcity, and Sensory Precision

At the other extreme are **deserts**, where temperatures can soar above 50 degrees Celsius during the day and plummet to near freezing at night. Water is scarce, and shelter is minimal, creating an environment where survival depends on acute sensory adaptations. Here, creatures have evolved to make the most of limited resources, relying on senses finely attuned to detect even the faintest traces of moisture or food.

The **camel** is a quintessential desert survivor. Known for its ability to endure long periods without water, the camel has not only physical adaptations—such as its hump, which stores fat for energy—but also remarkable sensory abilities. Camels have an exceptional sense of smell, allowing them to detect water sources from kilometres away. This ability is crucial in a landscape where finding water can mean the difference between life and death.

Another desert inhabitant, the **Namib Desert beetle**, has a unique way of collecting water. In the early morning, when the desert air cools, this beetle climbs to the top of a dune and positions itself so that its back faces into the breeze. Tiny bumps on its shell collect moisture from the fog, which then flows down into its mouth. This behaviour illustrates how even in the driest environments; life can adapt by using its senses to exploit every possible resource.

The stark conditions of the desert push these creatures to develop sensory abilities that we might find difficult to imagine. For them, survival is a daily struggle against the elements, and every sense must be honed to detect scarce resources, whether it's a distant water source or a brief window of cooler air.

High Altitudes: Thriving in Thin Air

In the thin air of the world's highest peaks, where oxygen levels drop dramatically, life faces a new set of challenges. For humans, ascending above 8,000 feet can lead to altitude sickness, with symptoms like shortness of breath, dizziness, and fatigue. Yet, some species have evolved to not only survive but thrive at altitudes where oxygen is scarce and temperatures are bitterly cold.

The **bar-headed goose** is known for its incredible migratory flights over the Himalayas, reaching altitudes of up to 29,000 feet—higher than Mount Everest. These birds have specially adapted haemoglobin that binds oxygen more efficiently, allowing them to endure the thin air at high altitudes. They also have larger lungs and more efficient breathing patterns, enabling them to sustain long flights in conditions that would overwhelm most other creatures.

Similarly, **yak**, which are native to the Tibetan Plateau, have large lung capacities and a high concentration of red blood cells, which allow them to live and graze at altitudes where oxygen is in short supply. Their thick fur protects them from the frigid temperatures, and their wide hooves provide stability on rocky, uneven terrain. These adaptations highlight the resilience of life and its ability to evolve specialized traits that meet the demands of high-altitude environments.

Caves: A World Without Light

In the pitch-black depths of **caves**, where sunlight never penetrates, life has taken on strange and fascinating forms. Without light, vision becomes irrelevant, and creatures must rely on other senses to navigate and find food. The **Mexican blind cavefish** is a striking example of how life can adapt to total darkness. Over generations, these fish have lost their eyesight, with their eye structures gradually degenerating as they adapted to life in perpetual darkness.

In place of vision, cavefish have evolved enhanced senses of touch and smell. They use specialized sensory cells in their skin to detect changes in water pressure, allowing them to "feel" their way through their environment. Another inhabitant of the dark, the **bat**, relies on echolocation to navigate and hunt. By emitting high-pitched sounds and listening to the returning echoes, bats create a mental map of their surroundings, detecting obstacles and prey with remarkable accuracy.

The creatures of caves reveal the extraordinary lengths to which life can adapt when traditional senses are rendered useless. They rely on sensory abilities that allow them to thrive in environments where sight and light are irrelevant, showcasing the diversity of perception that has evolved across different ecosystems.

Arctic Extremes: Cold, Darkness, and Survival

The **Arctic** presents one of the harshest environments on Earth, with temperatures that can plunge below -50 degrees Celsius, extended periods of darkness, and limited food supplies. Here, creatures must not only withstand the cold but also navigate a world where sensory perception is crucial for finding scarce resources.

The **polar bear** has a highly developed sense of smell, capable of detecting seals—a primary food source—up to a mile away, even through thick ice. This ability is essential in a habitat where food is often hidden beneath the frozen surface. **Arctic foxes** and **snowy owls** also possess keen senses of hearing and sight, allowing them to locate prey in low light conditions, where the landscape is blanketed in snow and ice.

The Arctic's inhabitants show us that even in the most extreme cold, life can develop sensory adaptations that turn inhospitable environments into survivable habitats. For them, survival is not just about withstanding the cold but about using their senses to locate food, detect predators, and navigate the frozen landscape.

Humans: Adapting Beyond Biology

While animals rely on biological adaptations to survive in extreme environments, humans have extended their reach through **technology**. Our survival is no longer solely tied to biological evolution; instead, we use tools and innovation to adapt to environments that would otherwise be inaccessible.

Through the use of deep-sea submersibles, we can explore the ocean's darkest depths, while satellites give us a view of Earth from space. **Infrared cameras** allow us to "see" heat, and **sonar systems** enable us to map the ocean floor. We have developed **oxygen tanks** to venture into high altitudes and **thermal suits** to withstand sub-zero temperatures. These technological adaptations allow us to extend our senses beyond their natural limits, enabling us to explore and understand environments that lie far beyond our biological capabilities.

In many ways, our technology serves as an extension of our perception, allowing us to interact with the world in ways that no other species can. This ability to adapt through innovation is a testament to the unique path of human evolution, demonstrating that survival can be achieved not just through biological change but through the power of ingenuity and invention.

Conclusion: Survival Through Perception and Adaptation

From the deepest ocean trenches to the highest mountain peaks, life has evolved remarkable ways to perceive and adapt to its surroundings. Whether it's the bioluminescent lure of the anglerfish, the echolocation of bats, or the advanced technology of humans, perception is at the heart of survival. Each organism experiences the world in a way that is uniquely suited to its environment, revealing the profound connection between adaptation and perception.

As we continue to explore the natural world, we are reminded that survival is not just about physical strength or endurance but about the ability to sense and respond to the environment. The diversity of life's perception showcases the resilience of nature, proving that in every environment, there is a way to adapt, evolve, and thrive.

"Survival is shaped not just by the world we live in, but by how we perceive it. From the deepest ocean trenches to the highest mountain peaks, life adapts, and with it, perception evolves to meet the demands of each environment."

Chapter 6: Dark Matter: The Universe's Hidden Skeleton

"Though unseen and undetectable by our instruments, dark matter weaves through the universe, silently shaping galaxies and holding the cosmos together. It is the invisible skeleton of reality, a force that hints at dimensions we have yet to explore."

The universe as we know it is held together by a force that remains largely invisible. This force, known as dark matter, makes up about 85% of the universe's total matter content, yet it does not emit, absorb, or reflect light. Dark matter's true nature eludes us, but its gravitational effects are undeniably real, providing a glimpse into a hidden framework that extends far beyond the visible stars and galaxies. It is, in many ways, the universe's hidden skeleton.

The Discovery of Dark Matter: A Ghostly Force

The concept of dark matter was first hinted at in the 1930s when astronomer **Fritz Zwicky** noticed that galaxies within the **Coma Cluster** were moving at speeds that defied Newtonian predictions. According to the gravitational forces of visible matter alone, these galaxies should have drifted apart. Yet, they remained tightly bound as though some unseen mass was holding them together. Zwicky termed this mysterious substance *dunkle Materie*—dark matter.

The notion lay dormant for several decades until **Vera Rubin** in the 1970s observed the rotation curves of spiral galaxies. According to Newton's laws, stars at the outer edges of a galaxy should move more slowly than those closer to the center. Yet, Rubin discovered that stars on the outskirts of galaxies moved just as fast as those near the core, suggesting an unseen gravitational pull. Thus, dark matter emerged not just as an idea but as an essential component of cosmic physics.

What Is Dark Matter Made Of? Candidates and Theories

Dark matter is profoundly elusive, and numerous theories have been proposed to explain its nature. Among the most popular candidates are **WIMPs** (Weakly Interacting Massive Particles). WIMPs are hypothesized to interact with regular matter only through gravity and possibly the weak nuclear force, making them difficult to detect. Scientists have spent decades trying to capture signs of WIMPs through underground detectors, yet they remain undetected, hinting that dark matter might be something even stranger.

Another candidate is the **axion**, a lightweight, hypothetical particle that could solve several problems in particle physics, including dark matter. Unlike WIMPs, axions are predicted to be exceptionally light and would interact with other particles at extremely low energies. Axions could also explain certain peculiarities in quantum mechanics, providing a bridge between dark matter and the subatomic world.

Some researchers have even proposed that dark matter may not be made of particles at all. Alternative theories, such as **Modified Newtonian Dynamics (MOND)**, suggest that the laws of gravity themselves might change at large scales. This theory posits that our understanding of gravity is incomplete, and what we perceive as dark matter could be a result of these misunderstood gravitational effects.

Dark Matter's Role in Sculpting the Universe

Dark matter doesn't just exist as a theoretical necessity; it plays an active role in shaping the cosmos. In the early universe, dark matter provided the scaffolding for galaxy formation. As the universe expanded after the **Big Bang**, dark matter began to clump together, creating massive gravitational wells. Ordinary matter, mostly hydrogen and helium, fell into these wells, eventually giving rise to the first stars and galaxies. Without dark matter, the universe would lack the intricate structure we see today.

The influence of dark matter extends beyond individual galaxies. It forms vast, invisible **filaments** that create a web-like structure across the universe. Galaxies are not distributed randomly; they are clustered along these filaments, forming a **cosmic web** that extends for billions of light-years. This structure, dictated by dark matter, defines the large-scale organization of the universe. In a way, dark matter acts as the architect of the cosmos, binding galaxies together and shaping their distribution on the grandest scales.

Dark Matter and the Hidden Dimensions Hypothesis

One of the most compelling theories about dark matter suggests that it could be linked to **higher dimensions**. While we experience reality in three spatial dimensions, theories like **string theory** propose the existence of additional dimensions that we cannot directly perceive. If dark matter primarily exists within these hidden dimensions, it would explain why it does not interact with regular matter in ways we can easily detect.

This idea suggests that dark matter particles might be like shadows of higher-dimensional objects, influencing our universe gravitationally but remaining invisible to our three-dimensional senses. Imagine a two-dimensional being living on a flat surface. If a three-dimensional object passes through their plane, they would only perceive a shadow or cross-section of that object. Similarly, we might be perceiving only the "shadow" of higher-dimensional entities, manifested as dark matter.

Such an idea challenges our very conception of space and time. If dark matter is connected to higher dimensions, then solving the mystery might reveal new aspects of reality, offering a glimpse into realms beyond human perception. This hypothesis also raises questions about the relationship between gravity and these hidden dimensions, suggesting that gravity could be weaker than other forces because it spreads across multiple dimensions.

Unravelling the Mystery: The Quest for Dark Matter Detection

The quest to detect dark matter has led to some of the most ambitious experiments in modern science. At the **Large Hadron Collider (LHC)**, scientists have been smashing particles together at nearly the speed of light, hoping to produce dark matter particles in the resulting collisions. The **XENON1T experiment**, located beneath the Italian Alps, seeks to capture signs of dark matter interacting with xenon atoms. Despite decades of research, however, dark matter has remained elusive, leading some to speculate that we may need entirely new methods or even a new understanding of physics to detect it.

Recent experiments have also hinted at unexpected results. In 2020, researchers at the **DAMA/LIBRA** experiment reported detecting an annual modulation in particle interactions, which they claim is consistent with the Earth moving through a dark matter halo. However, these findings remain controversial, and other labs have struggled to replicate them.

If dark matter does turn out to be composed of axions or some other exotic particle, future experiments may need to be even more sensitive, perhaps probing the universe at energies far below what current technology allows. It's possible that the discovery of dark matter will require a paradigm shift, one that could redefine our understanding of both the cosmos and the fundamental forces that govern it.

The Cosmic Web: Dark Matter as the Universe's Skeleton

On a grander scale, dark matter can be envisioned as the skeleton upon which the universe is built. This cosmic web of dark matter filaments holds galaxies in place and governs their movements, creating a structure that spans the entirety of the cosmos. These filaments act like the bones of a body, providing the framework that supports galaxies and galaxy clusters, binding the universe together in a way that visible matter alone could never accomplish.

But what if this cosmic web is more than just a physical structure? Some theorists speculate that the cosmic web could represent intersections of different dimensions, with dark matter serving as the glue that binds them together. If dark matter does indeed exist in higher dimensions, then the cosmic web could be a manifestation of interactions across these dimensions, connecting our universe to hidden realms of existence.

Conclusion: The Hidden Skeleton of Reality

Dark matter remains one of the greatest scientific mysteries of our time, a force that shapes the cosmos yet eludes our grasp. As scientists continue to search for it, dark matter beckons us to look beyond the visible and question the very nature of reality. Whether it is a particle, a wave, or a portal to other dimensions, dark matter is a reminder that the universe is more complex and mysterious than we can ever fully comprehend.

The journey to uncover dark matter's true nature is not just a quest to understand what lies beyond our reach but also a journey inward, challenging us to rethink our place in the cosmos and our understanding of the universe's hidden architecture. Whatever the outcome, the search for dark matter will undoubtedly reveal new insights, by transforming our view of reality and inviting us to explore the unseen forces that shape existence.

"Though unseen and undetectable by our instruments, dark matter weaves through the universe, silently shaping galaxies and holding the cosmos together. It is the invisible skeleton of reality, a force that hints at dimensions we have yet to explore."

Chapter 7: Magnetic Fields: The Unseen Forces of Navigation

"Magnetic fields, though invisible, shape our world and guide the movement of planets, animals, and even technology. These unseen forces offer a glimpse into the invisible architecture of nature and the cosmos."

Invisible to our senses but essential to our lives, magnetic fields permeate the universe, influencing everything from the smallest particles to entire galaxies. Though we rarely think about magnetic fields, their effects are constantly at work, quietly guiding the migration of birds, shielding Earth from solar winds, and even driving the motors in our everyday devices. They are the unseen forces of navigation, linking together worlds both large and small, tangible and intangible, physical and cosmic.

The Earth's Magnetic Shield: A Guardian Against Solar Winds

The Earth's magnetic field, generated by the swirling motion of molten iron within its core, acts as a giant protective shield known as the **magnetosphere**. Extending thousands of kilometres into space, this magnetic field deflects charged particles from the Sun, known as the **solar wind**. Without this shield, these particles would strip away Earth's atmosphere over time, making life as we know it impossible.

When solar winds collide with Earth's magnetosphere, they create stunning displays of light near the poles, known as the **aurora borealis** and **aurora australis**. These luminous curtains of colour are caused by charged particles interacting with gases in the atmosphere, producing flashes of green, red, and violet. But while beautiful, these auroras are also reminders of the magnetic field's role in protecting us from the Sun's more harmful effects.

Earth's magnetic field is far from static; it slowly drifts over time, with the magnetic poles gradually moving across the planet. Occasionally, these poles even **reverse**, flipping so that magnetic north becomes magnetic south. Such reversals, known as **geomagnetic reversals**, have occurred periodically throughout Earth's history, although scientists are still uncertain about the full impact of these events on the planet.

Magnetic Navigation: The Mystery of Animal Magnetoreception

While we may not be able to directly perceive magnetic fields, many animals possess an extraordinary ability to sense and respond to them. Known as **magnetoreception**, this ability is used by various species for navigation during long migrations. For instance, birds, sea turtles, and even certain insects have a magnetic sense that allows them to detect Earth's magnetic field and use it like a built-in compass.

The mechanisms behind magnetoreception remain largely mysterious. Some research suggests that birds may have magnetic-sensitive proteins in their eyes, enabling them to actually "see" magnetic fields as visual patterns. These proteins, called **cryptochromes**, may allow birds to orient themselves based on the Earth's magnetic field during their migrations.

Sea turtles are another fascinating example. After hatching on a beach, young turtles make an epic journey across the ocean, somehow finding their way back decades later to the exact same beach to lay their own eggs. Scientists believe that sea turtles may detect subtle variations in the Earth's magnetic field, enabling them to navigate with incredible precision over thousands of kilometres of open ocean.

But magnetoreception isn't limited to birds and turtles. **Honeybees** are known to use Earth's magnetic field to orient themselves while foraging for food. Some fish species, like the **salmon**, are believed to navigate using magnetic cues, guiding them as they swim upstream to their spawning grounds. This remarkable ability to sense magnetic fields is a reminder of the diversity of perception across species and the hidden ways in which life is interconnected with invisible forces.

Human Use of Magnetic Fields: From Ancient Compasses to Modern Technology

Humans have long relied on Earth's magnetic field for navigation. The invention of the **compass**, which dates back to ancient China, revolutionized sea travel by allowing sailors to determine their direction relative to the Earth's magnetic poles. This simple yet powerful tool enabled explorers to chart new courses, connect distant lands, and expand the boundaries of human civilization.

In modern times, we have learned to harness magnetic fields in even more sophisticated ways. **Magnetic Resonance Imaging (MRI)** machines, for example, use powerful magnetic fields to create detailed images of the body's internal structures. MRI scans align the hydrogen atoms in the body with a magnetic field, then disturb this alignment with a pulse of radio waves. As the atoms return to their original alignment, they emit signals that are captured and used to create highly detailed images, allowing doctors to diagnose diseases and injuries with remarkable precision.

Magnetic fields are also essential to the operation of **electric motors** and **generators**. In electric motors, magnetic fields interact with electric currents to produce motion, powering everything from household appliances to electric vehicles. In generators, the process is reversed: motion is used to create electricity through magnetic induction, a phenomenon discovered by **Michael Faraday** in the 19th century. This principle underlies much of the world's power generation, from hydroelectric dams to wind turbines.

Magnetars and Cosmic Magnetism: The Universe's Most Powerful Magnetic Fields

While the Earth's magnetic field is strong enough to protect us from solar winds, it pales in comparison to the magnetic fields found in certain astronomical objects. **Magnetars**, a type of neutron star, have the most intense magnetic fields known in the universe—trillions of times stronger than Earth's. These fields are so powerful that they can distort the shape of atoms, converting them into elongated, pencil-like forms. Magnetars are capable of emitting bursts of high-energy gamma rays and X-rays, creating some of the most violent events observed in space.

These cosmic magnetic fields are not only found around extreme objects like magnetars but also play a role in the larger structure of the universe. **Galaxies** and **galaxy clusters** are influenced by magnetic fields, which help to guide the movement of charged particles and influence the formation of stars. While we cannot directly observe these magnetic fields, their effects are visible in the behaviour of cosmic structures and the distribution of matter throughout the universe.

Interestingly, scientists are now exploring the possibility that magnetic fields may have influenced the **cosmic microwave background radiation**, the faint glow left over from the Big Bang. If true, magnetic fields could have shaped the very fabric of the universe in its earliest moments, leaving imprints on the distribution of galaxies and the structure of space-time itself.

The Quantum World of Magnetism: Spin and Electrons

On the smallest scales, magnetism is a result of quantum phenomena, particularly the property known as **spin**. Electrons, one of the fundamental particles of the universe, have a property called spin that gives rise to magnetic fields. When electrons spin in the same direction, they create a magnetic moment, which is why materials like **iron** become magnetized.

The quantum nature of magnetism also gives rise to fascinating phenomena like **superconductivity**. In certain materials, when cooled to very low temperatures, electrical resistance drops to zero, allowing electricity to flow without any loss of energy. Superconductors exhibit something known as the **Meissner effect**, where they repel magnetic fields, allowing them to levitate above magnets. This effect is being explored for applications in **maglev trains**, which use magnetic levitation to reduce friction and allow for high-speed travel.

The Future of Magnetic Fields: New Technologies and Potential Discoveries

As we continue to study magnetic fields, we are uncovering new ways to harness their power. **Fusion reactors**, which hold the promise of nearly limitless clean energy, rely on powerful magnetic fields to contain and control plasma at temperatures hotter than the core of the Sun. This technology could one day revolutionize energy production, providing a sustainable alternative to fossil fuels.

Magnetic fields are also being explored in **quantum computing**, where qubits—quantum bits of information—can be manipulated using magnetic fields. This could lead to breakthroughs in computational power, enabling us to solve problems that are currently intractable.

In addition, researchers are investigating how magnetic fields might influence **biological systems**. Some studies suggest that exposure to certain magnetic fields could have therapeutic effects, potentially aiding in the treatment of conditions like depression or chronic pain.

While still in the early stages, this research hints at the possibility of new medical treatments that harness the power of magnetism.

Conclusion: The Unseen Forces Shaping Our World

Magnetic fields are a reminder that much of reality operates beyond our immediate perception. These invisible forces shape the natural world, guide the movement of animals, power human technology, and even influence the cosmos. They are both ancient and modern, primal and cutting-edge, connecting us to the Earth and the stars.

By studying magnetic fields, we gain insight into the hidden architecture of nature and the universe. They show us that reality is filled with unseen forces, constantly at work in ways that stretch beyond the limits of our senses. As we continue to explore these magnetic mysteries, we are reminded that the world is far more complex, interconnected, and awe-inspiring than we could ever have imagined.

"Magnetic fields, though invisible, shape our world and guide the movement of planets, animals, and even technology. These unseen forces offer a glimpse into the invisible architecture of nature and the cosmos."

Chapter 8: Ecosystem Architects: Ants and Insects as Invisible Engineers

"Beneath our feet, armies of ants, termites, and other insects work tirelessly, shaping the environment in ways we often overlook. These tiny creatures are nature's hidden architects, playing vital roles in maintaining the balance of ecosystems."

Though they may be small, insects are among the most important creatures in the natural world. Often unseen and unappreciated, ants, termites, and other insects are essential architects of the ecosystems they inhabit. Through their tireless work, these tiny engineers perform tasks that are vital to the health of the environment, including aerating the soil, breaking down organic matter, and even cultivating crops.

Ants: The Builders, Farmers, and Caretakers

Ants are renowned for their complex societies and impressive engineering feats. A single ant colony can consist of millions of individuals, working in harmony to build nests that rival the sophistication of human cities. These nests, which may be located underground, within trees, or even in the canopies of rainforests, serve as hubs of activity, each chamber dedicated to a specific purpose. In some species, ants construct **tunnels that can extend**

for miles, providing ventilation and access to food, water, and nursery areas for the queen's offspring.

Ants are also skilled farmers. **Leafcutter ants**, found primarily in Central and South America, are famous for their practice of cultivating fungi. These ants cut leaves from nearby plants and carry them back to their nests, where they use them as a substrate to grow a specific type of fungus. The fungus serves as a food source for the colony, while the ants tend to the fungal garden with remarkable care, even using their own antimicrobial secretions to prevent meld growth. This intricate relationship demonstrates the ants' ability to not only modify their environment but to create and maintain their own agricultural systems.

Beyond their nests, ants are also influential in maintaining soil health. As they dig through the soil, ants aerate it, allowing water and nutrients to penetrate more deeply. This process is particularly important in tropical rainforests, where ants are among the primary agents of soil turnover, contributing to the health and diversity of plant life. Additionally, ants act as **seed dispersers** in many ecosystems. Certain plants produce seeds with nutrient-rich appendages called **elaiosomes**, which attract ants. The ants carry these seeds back to their nests, consuming the elaiosome and leaving the seed to germinate in a new location, thus aiding in the spread of plant species across the forest floor.

Termites: The Unsung Soil Engineers and Decomposers

While often viewed as pests, termites are critical to the health of many ecosystems. Termite mounds, found in tropical and subtropical regions, are architectural marvels, some reaching heights of over 30 feet. These towering structures are intricately designed to regulate temperature and humidity, providing a stable environment for the termite colony. Inside these mounds, termites create vast networks of tunnels and chambers, some of which are dedicated to cultivating fungi. Like ants, certain termite species grow their own fungal food, a practice that highlights their role as ecosystem engineers.

Termites are also essential decomposers. They feed on dead wood and other plant material, breaking down tough cellulose fibres that most other organisms cannot digest. By doing so, they recycle nutrients back into the soil, supporting the growth of plants and other organisms. In fact, termite activity is so crucial that in some ecosystems, they are responsible for recycling as much organic matter as all other decomposers combined. Without termites, dead plant material would accumulate, slowing nutrient cycling and potentially disrupting the balance of the ecosystem.

In arid regions, termites play an additional role as **water harvesters**. Their mounds can capture and retain moisture, creating microhabitats that support plants and other animals in otherwise dry environments. By enhancing soil structure and nutrient content, termites contribute to the fertility of these ecosystems, making them resilient to drought and other challenges.

The Ecological Impact of Insects on Biodiversity

Insects like ants and termites are more than just builders and decomposers; they are also key players in maintaining biodiversity. Their activities create habitats for other species, influence the distribution of plants, and support a wide range of animals, from small mammals to birds and reptiles. Ants, for example, are often involved in mutualistic relationships with other insects, such as **aphids**. The ants protect aphids from predators in exchange for the sugary honeydew that aphids produce. This relationship provides ants with a valuable food source while allowing aphids to thrive, demonstrating the interconnectedness of ecosystems.

Similarly, termites support a variety of species that depend on their mounds as shelter. Birds, reptiles, and small mammals often make their homes in abandoned termite mounds, finding refuge from predators and harsh environmental conditions. In some ecosystems, termite mounds act as **islands of biodiversity**, providing a stable microhabitat where plants and animals that would not otherwise survive can thrive.

Insects as Pollinators: The Silent Gardeners of Nature

While bees are often recognized as primary pollinators, many ants, beetles, and other insects also play important roles in pollination. **Ant pollination**, known as *myrmecophily*, is especially common in tropical and subtropical regions. Ants transfer pollen as they forage, allowing certain plant species to reproduce. Though less efficient than bees, ants still contribute significantly to plant reproduction, particularly in ecosystems where other pollinators are scarce.

Ants and other insects also act as **seed dispersers**, ensuring that plants can spread and colonize new areas. This process is particularly important in forest ecosystems, where seed dispersal helps maintain plant diversity and supports the regeneration of forests. By carrying seeds away from the parent plant, insects reduce competition and increase the likelihood that seeds will find suitable conditions for growth.

The role of insects in pollination and seed dispersal highlights their importance as **silent gardeners** of nature, supporting the health and diversity of ecosystems. Without these small creatures, many plants would struggle to reproduce, and the balance of life in these ecosystems would be profoundly disrupted.

The Interconnected World of Insect Engineers

The contributions of ants, termites, and other insects extend far beyond the immediate tasks they perform. By building nests, decomposing organic matter, pollinating plants, and dispersing seeds, these creatures shape the world around them in ways that are essential to the survival of countless other species. Their work creates habitats, recycles nutrients, and supports biodiversity, forming the backbone of ecosystems that sustain life on Earth.

In recent years, scientists have begun to appreciate the broader impact of these insect engineers. Research has shown that ecosystems with diverse insect populations are more resilient to environmental changes, such as climate fluctuations, habitat loss, and invasive species. The presence of insects like ants and termites helps to maintain the **ecological stability** of these systems, providing a buffer against disturbances and ensuring the continued health of the environment.

The Future of Ecosystems: Protecting Nature's Engineers

Despite their importance, insect populations are declining globally due to habitat destruction, pesticide use, and climate change. This decline poses a significant threat to ecosystems, as the loss of these tiny engineers could have ripple effects throughout the environment. Without ants, termites, and other insects, soil health would deteriorate, plant diversity would decrease, and the delicate balance of nature would be disrupted.

Conservation efforts aimed at protecting insect habitats and promoting biodiversity are crucial for the future of ecosystems. By understanding and valuing the roles that these small creatures play, we can take steps to preserve their habitats, reduce pesticide use, and restore ecosystems to support healthy insect populations. Protecting these invisible engineers is not only essential for the survival of the ecosystems they sustain but also for our own survival, as humans depend on the services that these ecosystems provide.

Conclusion: Insects as Architects of the Natural World

Ants, termites, and other insects are often overlooked, yet they are some of the most influential architects of the natural world. Through their tireless work, these tiny creatures maintain the balance of ecosystems, supporting the plants, animals, and fungi that depend on them. They are more than just insects; they are essential engineers, shaping the world in ways that are invisible but indispensable.

As we continue to explore and understand the hidden world of insects, we are reminded that the health of our planet depends on the contributions of all its inhabitants, no matter how small. By recognizing and protecting these unseen architects, we can ensure the continued resilience and diversity of the ecosystems that sustain life on Earth.

"Beneath our feet, armies of ants, termites, and other insects work tirelessly, shaping the environment in ways we often overlook. These tiny creatures are nature's hidden architects, playing vital roles in maintaining the balance of ecosystems."

Chapter 9: Sensing Through Sound: Echolocation and the World of Bats

"In a world where light is absent, sound becomes the guide. For creatures like bats, sound is more than just noise—it is a way to navigate, hunt, and understand their surroundings. In their darkness, they see through sound, revealing the unseen architecture of reality in a way that challenges our own limited perception."

While humans rely primarily on vision to perceive the world, there are other creatures whose understanding of reality is defined by a completely different sense—sound. For bats and other echolocating animals, sound is not just a means of communication but a primary way of navigating and interacting with their environment. Echolocation allows these animals to "see" using sound waves, an ability that grants them a unique perspective on the world, one that operates in the absence of light.

The Mechanics of Echolocation: Seeing with Sound

Echolocation is a fascinating sensory system that allows certain animals to emit sound waves and listen to the echoes that bounce back from objects in their environment. By analysing the timing and quality of these echoes, echolocating animals can determine the size, shape, distance, and even texture of objects around them. This ability is particularly useful for nocturnal creatures like bats, which rely on echolocation to hunt insects in the darkness of night.

The process begins when a bat emits a high-pitched call, often at frequencies above the range of human hearing. These sound waves travel through the air until they encounter an object, such as an insect or a tree. The waves then bounce back toward the bat, carrying information about the object they encountered. In a fraction of a second, the bat's brain processes this information, allowing it to create a mental map of its surroundings.

Bats are capable of producing up to **200 calls per second** while hunting, creating a continuous stream of information that enables them to track and capture fast-moving prey with incredible accuracy. Different species of bats use varying echolocation techniques, adapted to their specific environments and hunting styles. Some bats emit calls through their mouths, while others produce sounds through their nostrils, allowing them to fine-tune their echolocation abilities.

The Soundscape: Navigating an Invisible World

For echolocating animals, the world is made up of soundscapes—three-dimensional environments constructed entirely from sound. In these soundscapes, every surface, object, and living creature becomes part of a complex acoustic landscape. Bats can detect minute details within this soundscape, such as the fluttering wings of a moth or the surface texture of a leaf. In this way, they build a detailed picture of their surroundings that rivals the visual perception of sighted animals.

Echolocation is not limited to bats; it is also used by other animals that navigate challenging environments. **Dolphins**, for example, use echolocation to navigate the dark waters of the ocean and locate fish. By emitting clicks and listening to the echoes, dolphins can perceive underwater structures and track the movements of other animals, even in murky or pitch-black conditions.

Interestingly, dolphins are able to adjust the frequency and intensity of their clicks depending on the task at hand. When exploring an open area, they use broad, low-frequency clicks that cover a wide range. But when focusing on a specific target, they switch to high-frequency clicks that provide more detail. This ability to customize their echolocation signals demonstrates the versatility and sophistication of echolocation as a sensory tool.

The Superpowers of Echolocating Animals: Beyond Sound

While echolocation allows animals to navigate in darkness, some species have evolved additional abilities that make them even more adept at using sound. Bats, for instance, can not only hear the echoes of their calls but also detect subtle changes in the pitch and volume of these echoes. This enables them to gauge the speed and direction of moving prey with astonishing precision.

Moreover, many bats can emit sounds that are beyond the hearing range of their prey, allowing them to hunt without alerting their targets. In some species, bats have evolved **ultrasonic calls** that are so high-pitched that only they can hear them. This creates an invisible and silent battlefield in which the bat has a distinct advantage over its prey.

In a more extreme example, **toothed whales** like the sperm whale have developed echolocation abilities powerful enough to stun or disorient their prey. By producing exceptionally loud clicks, these whales can generate sound waves that overwhelm the senses of nearby fish and squid, making them easier to catch. This use of echolocation as a weapon demonstrates the extraordinary potential of sound as a tool for survival and hunting.

Echolocation and the Evolution of Hearing: A Marvel of Adaptation

The evolution of echolocation highlights the incredible adaptability of nature. Bats, dolphins, and other echolocating animals have evolved specialized auditory systems that allow them to process sound with remarkable speed and accuracy. In bats, for instance, the **inner ear** contains highly sensitive cells that can detect even the faintest echoes, while the brain is equipped with neural pathways dedicated to processing echolocation signals in real-time.

For dolphins and other marine mammals, echolocation requires additional adaptations to account for the unique properties of sound in water. Sound travels faster and farther in water than in air, so these animals have evolved structures like the **melon**, a specialized organ in the forehead that focuses sound waves. By adjusting the shape of the melon, dolphins can fine-tune their echolocation calls, allowing them to locate objects with pinpoint accuracy.

Interestingly, some researchers believe that early humans may have possessed a rudimentary form of echolocation. Blind individuals, for example, have been known to develop a form of "clicking" echolocation, using tongue clicks and listening to the echoes to navigate their surroundings. While this ability is nowhere near as refined as that of bats or dolphins, it suggests that the human brain may have untapped potential when it comes to interpreting sound as a spatial sense.

The Science of Echolocation: Lessons for Technology

Echolocation has inspired a range of human technologies, from **sonar** to **ultrasound imaging**. Sonar, used by submarines and ships, operates on the same principle as echolocation, emitting sound waves and analysing the returning echoes to detect objects underwater. This technology has been invaluable for navigation, exploration, and even detecting underwater hazards.

Ultrasound imaging, commonly used in medical diagnostics, is another technology that relies on echolocation principles. By emitting high-frequency sound waves and capturing the echoes, ultrasound machines create detailed images of internal organs, allowing doctors to diagnose conditions without invasive procedures. In this way, echolocation has provided a model for human innovations that enhance our own abilities to perceive and interact with the world.

As we continue to develop new technologies, echolocation remains a source of inspiration for fields like **robotics** and **artificial intelligence**. Scientists are exploring ways to integrate echolocation into autonomous vehicles, enabling them to navigate complex environments by detecting obstacles and mapping their surroundings through sound. This approach could prove especially useful in environments where visual cues are unreliable or unavailable, such as underground mines or deep-sea exploration.

The Possibility of Human Echolocation: Unlocking Hidden Senses

While echolocation is not a natural ability for humans, there are individuals who have learned to use sound as a way of navigating their environment. Some visually impaired people have developed the ability to create mental maps through a form of human echolocation, using clicks, snaps, or taps to produce echoes. By listening to these echoes, they can detect obstacles, judge distances, and even identify objects around them.

Research into human echolocation has revealed that the human brain can adapt to process echoes in much the same way as it processes visual information. Studies have shown that echolocators engage the **visual cortex** of the brain when interpreting echoes, suggesting that the brain can repurpose unused neural pathways to develop new senses. This phenomenon, known as **neuroplasticity**, underscores the brain's remarkable capacity for adaptation and highlights the potential for humans to expand their sensory experiences in novel ways.

Conclusion: The Hidden World of Sound

Echolocation opens a window into a hidden world of perception that challenges our understanding of reality. For animals like bats and dolphins, sound provides access to a dimension of reality that is beyond the reach of human vision. These creatures remind us that our perception of the world is limited by the senses we possess, and that there may be other ways of experiencing reality that are as vivid and detailed as sight.

As we continue to explore the mysteries of echolocation, we gain new insights into the adaptability of life and the ways in which different species have evolved to navigate their environments. By studying these extraordinary animals, we not only learn more about the natural world but also expand our own horizons, considering new possibilities for perception and understanding. Echolocation serves as a reminder that reality is far richer and more complex than we can ever fully perceive, inviting us to imagine what other hidden worlds might lie just beyond our reach.

"In a world where light is absent, sound becomes the guide. For creatures like bats, sound is more than just noise—it is a way to navigate, hunt, and understand their surroundings. In their darkness, they see through sound, revealing the unseen architecture of reality in a way that challenges our own limited perception."

Chapter 10: In the Deep: Life in the Abyss

"Far below the ocean's surface lies a world of darkness, pressure, and isolation. In this harsh, alien environment, life has adapted in extraordinary ways to survive the depths."

The deep ocean remains one of the most mysterious and least explored regions on our planet. Stretching miles below the surface, it is a place of eternal darkness, immense pressure, and cold temperatures that hover just above freezing. Despite these harsh conditions, the deep sea is teeming with life—organisms that have evolved to withstand the extreme challenges of the abyssal world.

This chapter takes us on a journey into the deep, where bioluminescent creatures light up the dark, strange fish with otherworldly adaptations hunt in silence, and ecosystems flourish around scorching hydrothermal vents. In this hidden realm, survival is a testament to the resilience and adaptability of life in even the most inhospitable places.

The Abyssal Zone: A World Without Sunlight

The ocean can be divided into several distinct zones, each with its own unique conditions and inhabitants.

Beyond the reach of sunlight lies the **abyssal zone**, ranging from 4,000 to 6,000 meters below the surface. Here, in a world of perpetual darkness, photosynthesis is impossible, and life depends on other sources of energy. Despite the absence of light, the abyssal zone is far from empty. Creatures here have adapted to make the most of scarce resources, evolving specialized strategies to find food and avoid predators.

One of the most remarkable adaptations of deep-sea life is **bioluminescence**—the ability to produce light. Many deep-sea animals, from jellyfish to fish to squid, possess light-producing organs that allow them to glow in the dark. Some use bioluminescence to attract prey, while others use it to communicate or camouflage themselves against the faint light filtering down from above. The result is a dazzling array of twinkling lights that illuminate the darkness, creating an eerie but beautiful undersea light show.

For example, the **lanternfish**, one of the most common fish in the deep sea, is named for the tiny lights that cover its body. These lights help the fish blend in with the faint light above, making it nearly invisible to predators lurking below. On the other hand, predators like the **anglerfish** use a bioluminescent lure to attract unsuspecting prey. This infamous fish dangles a glowing appendage in front of its mouth, luring other fish close enough to be snapped up in a flash.

Surviving the Pressure: Nature's Master Engineers

At depths of several thousand meters, the pressure is hundreds of times greater than at the surface—enough to crush most surface-dwelling organisms. Yet, the creatures that inhabit the deep have evolved remarkable adaptations to survive these crushing forces. Many deep-sea animals, like the **snailfish**, have bodies that are almost gelatinous, with no air-filled cavities that would collapse under pressure. This allows them to withstand the immense weight of the water above.

In the **hadal zone**, the deepest part of the ocean found in trenches like the Mariana Trench, pressures can reach over 1,000 times that at sea level. Yet, even here, life thrives. Species such as **amphipods** and **sea cucumbers** have adapted to these extreme conditions. Their cells contain high levels of **trimethylamine oxide (TMAO)**, a compound that helps stabilize proteins under high pressure, allowing their bodies to function normally despite the crushing depths.

Interestingly, recent studies have revealed that some deep-sea creatures possess enzymes that are uniquely adapted to function in high-pressure environments. These **barophilic enzymes** allow metabolic processes to continue efficiently, enabling organisms to survive and even thrive in the hadal zone. The discovery of such enzymes has sparked interest in their potential applications in biotechnology, as they could lead to the development of industrial processes that operate under extreme conditions.

The Deep-Sea Food Web: Thriving in an Ecosystem of Scarcity

Without sunlight to fuel photosynthesis, life in the deep ocean relies on other sources of energy. Most organisms in the abyssal zone depend on **marine snow**, a continuous shower of organic material that drifts down from the upper layers of the ocean. This "snow" is made up of dead plankton, algae, faecal pellets, and other detritus, providing a vital source of nutrients for scavengers and filter feeders on the ocean floor.

Some of the most famous scavengers in the deep sea are **hagfish**, eel-like creatures that feed on carcasses that have fallen to the ocean floor. Hagfish use their tooth-like structures to burrow into the flesh of dead animals, consuming them from the inside out. Other creatures, like **giant isopods**, feast on the remains of fish and other animals that sink to the bottom, playing a crucial role in recycling nutrients in the deep-sea ecosystem.

In addition to marine snow, some deep-sea organisms have evolved to take advantage of **chemosynthesis**, a process that allows certain bacteria to convert chemicals like hydrogen sulphide into energy. This process is most famously associated with hydrothermal vent communities, where superheated water rich in minerals gushes out of cracks in the ocean floor, creating an oasis of life in the otherwise barren deep sea.

Hydrothermal Vents: Oases of Life in the Abyss

Discovered in 1977, **hydrothermal vents** are some of the most extraordinary ecosystems on Earth. These vents are found along mid-ocean ridges, where tectonic plates are moving apart and molten rock rises to the surface. As seawater seeps into the crust and encounters hot magma, it becomes superheated and rich in minerals, eventually spewing back into the ocean through vents, creating plumes of hot, mineral-laden water.

Despite the extreme conditions, hydrothermal vents are home to thriving communities of organisms. Giant **tube worms** are among the most iconic inhabitants of these vents. These worms, which can grow up to two meters in length, lack a digestive system and instead rely on a symbiotic relationship with **chemosynthetic bacteria**. The bacteria live inside the tube worms and convert hydrogen sulphide from the vent water into energy, which sustains the worms.

Hydrothermal vents are also inhabited by a variety of other species, including **vent crabs**, **vent shrimp**, and **vent clams**. These organisms have evolved to tolerate high temperatures, toxic chemicals, and low oxygen levels, making them some of the most resilient creatures on the planet. The discovery of life around hydrothermal vents has revolutionized our understanding of the conditions that can support life and has even fuelled speculation about the potential for similar ecosystems on other planets and moons.

Cold Seeps: Another Hidden World of Chemosynthetic Life

In addition to hydrothermal vents, the deep sea is also home to **cold seeps**, areas where methane and other hydrocarbons seep from the ocean floor. Unlike hydrothermal vents, cold seeps are not associated with volcanic activity, and the water around them is near freezing. However, like vents, cold seeps support unique ecosystems that rely on chemosynthesis rather than photosynthesis.

At cold seeps, bacteria that consume methane and hydrogen sulphide form the basis of the food web. These bacteria are often found in symbiotic relationships with larger organisms, such as **mussels** and **tubeworms**, which provide a stable habitat for the bacteria in exchange for nutrients. Cold seeps are also home to **methane ice worms**, which live on frozen methane deposits and feed on chemosynthetic bacteria.

Cold seeps, like hydrothermal vents, demonstrate the diversity of life in the deep sea and the ability of organisms to adapt to extreme and isolated environments. They also provide valuable insights into the potential for life in similar environments on other worlds, such as Jupiter's moon Europa, which is believed to have subsurface oceans that could harbor chemosynthetic life.

The Fascination of the Deep: What Lies Beneath

The deep sea is not only a realm of scientific interest but also a source of endless fascination for explorers and adventurers. Despite the advances in technology, only a fraction of the ocean floor has been explored, and each new expedition reveals strange and unexpected discoveries. **Deep-sea exploration vehicles**, like remotely operated vehicles (ROVs) and submersibles, have allowed scientists to descend into the depths and capture images of alien-like creatures and landscapes that are as captivating as they are mysterious.

Exploring the deep ocean presents unique challenges, not least because of the intense pressure and darkness. However, it is precisely these challenges that make the deep sea so intriguing. With each new discovery, we learn more about the resilience of life and the adaptability of organisms to extreme environments. The deep sea serves as a reminder that our planet is still full of uncharted territories and that the natural world holds secrets yet to be revealed.

Conclusion: The Resilience of Life in the Abyss

The deep sea is a testament to the extraordinary adaptability of life. In an environment where sunlight cannot reach, pressure is immense, and food is scarce, organisms have evolved remarkable strategies to survive. From bioluminescent fish that light up the darkness to chemosynthetic bacteria that thrive on chemical energy, the deep sea is a world of innovation and resilience.

As we continue to explore the abyss, we are reminded of the vastness and complexity of our planet and the incredible diversity of life that exists within it. The creatures of the deep sea challenge our understanding of the limits of life and inspire us to imagine what other hidden worlds might lie beyond our reach. In the darkness of the deep ocean, life flourishes against all odds, revealing that even the most extreme environments are teeming with life.

"Far below the ocean's surface lies a world of darkness, pressure, and isolation. In this harsh, alien environment, life has adapted in extraordinary ways to survive the depths."

Chapter 11: The Human Microbiome: Invisible Partners in Survival

"Within each of us resides a vast, invisible world of microorganisms that play an essential role in our health, survival, and even our behaviour. These unseen partners — the human microbiome — are as vital to our existence as our own cells."

When we think of life, we tend to think about the tangible aspects—our organs, tissues, and cells. But in reality, each human being is a complex ecosystem teeming with trillions of microorganisms, collectively known as the human microbiome. These microscopic allies include bacteria, viruses, fungi, and even archaea, and they are essential to our survival in ways that are only now beginning to be understood.

The microbiome is not just a collection of passengers; it is an active, dynamic network that influences almost every aspect of our health. Without it, our bodies would struggle to perform basic functions, from digesting food to fighting off infections. In fact, we are more microbial than human, with the number of microbial cells in our bodies outnumbering human cells by an astonishing ratio. And while this might sound unsettling, it's a reminder that survival itself is a collaborative effort, involving partnerships that reach down to the microscopic level.

In this chapter, we explore the human microbiome, its diverse ecosystems, and the ways it influences our bodies, minds, and behaviours. By diving into this unseen world, we uncover the hidden layers of life within us, and begin to appreciate the intricate web of connections that sustain our existence.

The Microscopic City Within

The human body is host to a staggering 100 trillion microbial cells, distributed across various regions, each forming unique ecosystems. The gut, home to the largest collection of these organisms, contains over 1,000 different species of bacteria. Other regions, like the skin, mouth, and even lungs, harbor distinct communities, each adapted to its specific environment. These microscopic ecosystem's function much like a bustling city, with each species performing specialized tasks that contribute to the overall health and stability of their host.

The diversity of the microbiome is astounding. In the gut alone, microbial diversity rivals that of a tropical rainforest, with thousands of species interacting in a delicate balance. This diversity is crucial because different species perform different functions—some break down complex carbohydrates, others produce essential vitamins, and still others help regulate the immune system. The more diverse the microbiome, the more resilient it tends to be, capable of adapting to changes and resisting harmful pathogens.

Our microbiome is as unique as a fingerprint, shaped by factors like genetics, diet, lifestyle, and even where we live. This individuality means that the microbial ecosystem in one person's gut can be vastly different from another's. And while some microbial species are common across all humans, many are specific to each individual, forming a microbial signature that reflects their unique journey through life.

The Gut-Brain Connection: Microbes and the Mind

In recent years, scientists have discovered an astonishing connection between the gut microbiome and the brain, known as the **gut-brain axis**. It turns out that the microbes in our digestive system can influence our mood, cognition, and even our behaviour. How? By producing neurotransmitters—chemical messengers like serotonin and dopamine that are crucial for regulating emotions and mental processes.

Around 90% of the body's serotonin, often dubbed the "feel-good" hormone, is produced in the gut. This means that the microbes residing in our intestines have a significant influence on how we feel. Disruptions to the gut microbiome have been linked to mental health conditions like anxiety, depression, and even conditions such as autism spectrum disorders. In one study, scientists found that transplanting the gut microbiome from a person with depression into a healthy individual could induce depressive-like symptoms, suggesting a direct causal link between gut health and mood.

While this field of research is still evolving, it opens up exciting possibilities for new treatments. Imagine treating depression or anxiety by modifying the gut microbiome, rather than relying solely on medications that target the brain. The gut-brain connection challenges our understanding of mental health and highlights the profound influence that our microscopic companions have on our minds.

Training Our Immune System: Microbes as Teachers

From birth, the microbiome plays a crucial role in training the immune system. As soon as we are born, microbes begin colonizing our bodies, and this early exposure is essential for teaching our immune system to distinguish between friend and foe. The interactions between microbes and immune cells help to build a strong, balanced immune system that can protect against infections without overreacting to harmless substances.

Research has shown that children who grow up in environments rich in microbial diversity, such as farms or rural areas, have lower rates of allergies and autoimmune diseases. This is known as the **hygiene hypothesis**, which suggests that exposure to a wide variety of microbes helps the immune system develop tolerance. Conversely, children in overly sanitized environments may have underexposed immune systems, increasing their risk of developing allergies and other immune-related disorders.

In addition to training the immune system, the microbiome acts as a first line of defence against harmful pathogens. Beneficial microbes compete with harmful bacteria for space and nutrients, a phenomenon known as **colonization resistance**. By maintaining a healthy balance, the microbiome helps keep potential invaders at bay and prevents infections before they even begin.

Antibiotics: A Double-Edged Sword

Antibiotics have saved countless lives by effectively killing harmful bacteria, but they can also disrupt the delicate balance of the microbiome. When we take antibiotics, we don't just target the pathogens; we also wipe out beneficial bacteria that are essential for our health. This disruption can lead to **dysbiosis**, a condition where harmful bacteria flourish due to the absence of beneficial competitors.

Dysbiosis has been linked to a wide range of health problems, from digestive disorders like irritable bowel syndrome (IBS) to skin conditions, mental health issues, and even metabolic diseases like obesity and diabetes. Moreover, the overuse of antibiotics has contributed to the rise of **antibiotic-resistant bacteria**, which pose a serious global health threat. When beneficial bacteria are destroyed, resistant pathogens can take over, leading to infections that are increasingly difficult to treat.

To protect our microbiome, it is essential to use antibiotics responsibly and support the health of beneficial microbes. Diet plays a significant role in this. Foods's rich in fiber, such as fruits, vegetables, and whole grains, provide nourishment for beneficial gut bacteria, helping them thrive. Probiotic-rich foods, like yogurt, kefir, and sauerkraut, can also help replenish beneficial bacteria, especially after antibiotic use.

The Microbiome and Human Evolution

The relationship between humans and their microbiome is not a recent development—it has been shaped over millions of years of evolution. Some scientists even suggest that we have evolved to be dependent on our microbial partners, as they provide essential functions that our own bodies cannot perform. For example, certain gut bacteria help break down dietary fiber into short-chain fatty acids, which serve as a vital energy source for the cells lining our intestines.

Moreover, the microbiome may have influenced our evolutionary path in more subtle ways. For example, some researchers speculate that our ancestors' diets shaped their microbiomes, which in turn may have influenced their development, health, and survival. The diverse diets of hunter-gatherer societies, rich in plant fibres, likely promoted a more diverse microbiome, which could have conferred health benefits that aided in survival and adaptation.

Understanding the microbiome's role in human evolution provides valuable insights into our present-day health. Modern diets, often high in processed foods and low in fiber, may not provide the necessary nutrients to support a diverse and balanced microbiome, potentially contributing to the rise in chronic diseases.

A World Within: The Ethical and Philosophical Implications

The discovery of the microbiome challenges our traditional notions of self. If our bodies are composed of as many microbial cells as human cells, then what does it mean to be human? Are we individuals, or are we communities of life forms working together for mutual benefit? This realization blurs the boundaries between "us" and "them" and invites us to reconsider our place in the natural world.

Moreover, the microbiome has ethical implications, particularly when it comes to medical treatments. As scientists explore therapies that involve altering the microbiome—such as faecal transplants or probiotic interventions—they must grapple with questions about the long-term effects of these treatments and the potential consequences of manipulating such a complex ecosystem.

Conclusion: Embracing Our Invisible Partners

The human microbiome is a vital part of who we are, influencing everything from digestion and immunity to mood and behaviour. These invisible partners remind us that survival is not a solitary Endeavor but a collaborative process involving countless organisms that live within us. As we continue to explore the microbiome, we uncover new layers of interconnectedness, revealing that our health and well-being are deeply tied to the invisible world that inhabits us.

In the end, the microbiome teaches us a profound lesson about life—that we are not isolated beings but part of a vast web of relationships, where even the smallest organisms play crucial roles. By embracing our microbiome, we can take proactive steps to nurture our health, recognizing that the secret to well-being lies not only in our own hands but also in the unseen world within.

"Within each of us resides a vast, invisible world of microorganisms that play an essential role in our health, survival, and even our behaviour. These unseen partners — the human microbiome — are as vital to our existence as our own cells."

Chapter 12: Cosmic Waves: The Power of Invisible Radiation

"Invisible to the eye, yet powerful enough to shape the cosmos, cosmic waves—radiation that travels through the universe—connect galaxies, stars, and planets. They move silently through space, carrying the energy of the stars, revealing a hidden reality that we can barely comprehend."

When we gaze up at the night sky, we see the visible light from stars and galaxies, but this light is only a fraction of the energy that permeates the universe. A far more significant portion of the universe's energy travels as invisible radiation, in the form of cosmic waves that traverse the vast distances of space. These waves, spanning a spectrum from low-energy radio waves to high-energy gamma rays, carry with them the energy and information of the cosmos, silently weaving through the fabric of reality.

Despite being invisible to our senses, these cosmic waves reveal a hidden world, one that can only be detected with the aid of advanced technology. The energy they carry shapes the formation of galaxies, the behaviour of black holes, and even the fundamental properties of matter itself. They are a testament to the complexity and interconnectedness of the universe, hinting at forces and dimensions that we can barely comprehend.

In this chapter, we will explore the nature of cosmic waves and the profound impact they have on the universe. From the faint whisper of radio waves to the violent bursts of gamma rays, we will uncover the hidden architecture of reality, gaining insights into the forces that govern the cosmos.

The Electromagnetic Spectrum: Unveiling Invisible Waves

The electromagnetic spectrum encompasses all forms of electromagnetic radiation, ranging from long-wavelength radio waves to short-wavelength gamma rays. Our eyes are sensitive to only a small portion of this spectrum—the visible light that allows us to see the world around us. But beyond this narrow band lies a vast array of invisible radiation, each type carrying different energy levels and interacting with matter in unique ways.

- **Radio Waves**: These are the longest waves in the spectrum, with wavelengths that can span from a few millimetres to hundreds of kilometres. They carry signals across the universe, allowing us to detect objects like pulsars, distant galaxies, and even the remnants of the Big Bang. Radio waves can travel vast distances, making them ideal for exploring the farthest reaches of the cosmos.
- **Microwaves**: With shorter wavelengths than radio waves, microwaves are associated with cosmic phenomena like the Cosmic Microwave Background (CMB). The CMB is a faint glow that fills the entire universe, representing the afterglow of the Big Bang. It provides a snapshot of the universe as it was nearly 13.8 billion years ago, offering insights into its early development.

- **Infrared Radiation**: Often associated with heat, infrared radiation reveals information about the temperatures of celestial objects. By observing the infrared spectrum, scientists can peer through cosmic dust clouds to study the formation of stars and planetary systems, which are hidden from view in visible light.
- **Ultraviolet Radiation**: Though invisible to us, ultraviolet (UV) radiation is highly energetic and capable of causing chemical reactions. It plays a crucial role in the formation of stars and the evolution of galaxies. Observing UV radiation allows astronomers to study hot, young stars and the regions of intense star formation.
- **X-rays**: These waves penetrate dense matter, allowing us to study high-energy phenomena like black holes, neutron stars, and supernova remnants. X-ray telescopes capture emissions from some of the most energetic events in the universe, helping us understand the extreme environments where matter and energy interact under intense gravitational forces.
- **Gamma Rays**: At the highest end of the spectrum, gamma rays carry enormous amounts of energy. They are produced by the most violent events in the cosmos, such as the collision of neutron stars, gamma-ray bursts, and the annihilation of matter and antimatter. Gamma rays provide a glimpse into the universe's most explosive and mysterious events, revealing insights into phenomena that lie at the frontier of our understanding.

Each of these waves represents a different aspect of cosmic energy, and by studying them, scientists are able to peel back the layers of the universe, gaining insights into forces and processes that are hidden from visible light.

The Cosmic Microwave Background: Echoes of the Big Bang

One of the most profound discoveries in cosmology is the Cosmic Microwave Background (CMB), a faint glow of radiation that fills the universe and serves as a remnant of the Big Bang. Discovered in 1965 by Arno Penzias and Robert Wilson, the CMB provides a snapshot of the universe when it was just 380,000 years old—a mere infant in cosmic terms.

The CMB is not just a relic of the past; it is a window into the conditions that shaped the early universe. By studying the subtle variations in the CMB, scientists have been able to reconstruct the universe's early structure, revealing the distribution of matter and energy at the moment when the first atoms began to form. These variations are like cosmic fingerprints, telling the story of how galaxies, stars, and planets would later emerge.

What makes the CMB even more fascinating is that it exists in the microwave portion of the spectrum, completely invisible to human eyes. To detect it, scientists use specialized instruments that can capture microwaves, allowing them to study the faint afterglow of creation. In this sense, the CMB is a testament to the power of invisible radiation, providing us with a direct link to the origins of the cosmos.

Gamma Rays and the Universe's Most Violent Events

While the CMB offers a glimpse into the universe's infancy, gamma rays provide insights into its most violent and energetic phenomena. These high-energy waves are produced by cataclysmic events such as supernovae, gamma-ray bursts, and black hole mergers. Gamma-ray bursts, for instance, are the most powerful explosions known to occur, releasing as much energy in a few seconds as the Sun will emit over its entire 10-billion-year lifespan.

Gamma rays reveal the universe's extremes, from the collapse of massive stars to the formation of black holes. Because they can pass through dense matter, gamma rays allow scientists to study events that are otherwise hidden from view. They are key to understanding the life cycles of stars, the formation of neutron stars, and the mysterious behaviour of black holes, where gravity and quantum mechanics intersect in ways that challenge our understanding of physics.

By studying gamma rays, scientists are also probing the limits of the known universe, exploring phenomena that occur billions of light-years away. These distant explosions and collisions send gamma rays across the cosmos, providing us with glimpses into the most energetic processes in existence.

The Invisible Architecture of the Universe

Cosmic waves reveal a hidden architecture that shapes the universe at every level. Radio waves map the distribution of galaxies, X-rays unveil the hot, dense regions around black holes, and gamma rays expose the universe's most explosive events. Together, they create a multidimensional picture of the cosmos, one that is far richer and more complex than what we can perceive with our eyes alone.

Invisible radiation also reveals the influence of forces that are not fully understood, such as dark matter and dark energy. While dark matter does not emit any form of radiation, its gravitational effects can be detected by the way it shapes the distribution of cosmic waves. Similarly, dark energy—an enigmatic force that is causing the universe to expand at an accelerating rate—leaves subtle imprints on the distribution of cosmic radiation, hinting at its role in the evolution of the cosmos.

The study of cosmic waves has shown that the universe is a vast, interconnected web, with energy and matter flowing through invisible channels. These channels connect galaxies, form stars, and create the conditions necessary for life. In this sense, cosmic waves are the veins of the universe, carrying the energy that sustains it.

The Quest for Hidden Dimensions

As scientists probe deeper into the mysteries of cosmic radiation, they are also exploring the possibility of hidden dimensions. Gravitational waves, for instance, are ripples in spacetime caused by the movement of massive objects. Unlike electromagnetic waves, which travel through space, gravitational waves stretch and compress space itself, revealing the dynamic nature of the cosmos.

Some theories suggest that gravitational waves could be influenced by extra dimensions—hidden realms that lie beyond our perception. If these dimensions exist, they could hold the key to understanding the fundamental forces that govern the universe, from gravity to electromagnetism. Detecting these hidden dimensions would require even more advanced technology, but the possibility of their existence hints at a reality that is far richer than we currently understand.

The Role of Technology: Expanding Our Vision

The study of cosmic waves would be impossible without the aid of technology. From radio telescopes that capture the faint signals of distant galaxies to satellites that detect X-rays and gamma rays, technology has extended our reach, allowing us to perceive the invisible forces that shape the universe.

In recent years, advancements in imaging and data processing have revolutionized our ability to study cosmic radiation. Instruments like the Hubble Space Telescope, the Chandra X-ray Observatory, and the Fermi Gamma-ray Space Telescope have provided unprecedented views of the cosmos, revealing phenomena that were once beyond our comprehension.

As technology continues to advance, it will open up new frontiers of exploration, allowing us to detect even more subtle forms of radiation and possibly even the effects of hidden dimensions. With each new discovery, we gain a deeper understanding of the universe and our place within it, pushing the boundaries of perception ever further.

Conclusion: Unseen Waves, Hidden Realities

Cosmic waves are the silent architects of the universe, shaping the cosmos in ways that are invisible to the human eye. They carry the energy of the stars, reveal the remnants of the Big Bang, and expose the universe's most violent events. By studying these waves, we are able to perceive a hidden reality, one that is filled with forces and dimensions that lie beyond our understanding.

As we continue to explore the electromagnetic spectrum and beyond, we are reminded that the universe is far more complex and mysterious than we can comprehend. The invisible radiation that permeates the cosmos hints at a reality that is richer and more interconnected than we can perceive. In the end, cosmic waves are a testament to the power of the unseen, revealing a universe that is filled with hidden beauty and wonder.

"Invisible to the eye, yet powerful enough to shape the cosmos, cosmic waves—radiation that travels through the universe—connect galaxies, stars, and planets. They move silently through space, carrying the energy of the stars, revealing a hidden reality that we can barely comprehend."

Chapter 13: Time Perception: The Hidden Dimension

"Time is the one dimension we cannot escape. It is the thread that weaves through every moment of existence, yet its true nature remains elusive. From the ticking of a clock to the lifespan of stars, time reveals itself in ways that challenge our understanding of reality."

We are all bound by time, yet it is a concept that eludes precise definition. Time shapes every aspect of existence, from the fleeting moment of a single heartbeat to the vast cosmic eras over which galaxies are born, grow, and fade. But what is time? Is it merely a tool we use to sequence events, or does it have an independent existence, woven into the very fabric of the universe?

As we delve deeper into the mystery of time, we find that it is far more complex than we might imagine. Time can be stretched, compressed, and even stopped under certain conditions. It is intimately linked to space, and together they form the framework within which all physical phenomena occur. Yet, despite centuries of scientific inquiry and philosophical contemplation, time remains one of the greatest enigmas of existence.

This chapter explores time as a hidden dimension, one that shapes our reality but remains largely beyond our grasp. We will journey from the human experience of time to the dizzying implications of time dilation, the possibility of time travel, and the concept of a multidimensional universe where time may behave in ways we cannot yet comprehend.

The Fabric of Spacetime: A New Perspective on Reality

In the early 20th century, Albert Einstein revolutionized our understanding of time with his theories of special and general relativity. According to Einstein, time is not an isolated entity; it is inextricably linked to space, forming a four-dimensional structure known as spacetime. In this model, massive objects like planets and stars create curves in the fabric of spacetime, resulting in what we perceive as gravity.

But gravity also affects the passage of time. This phenomenon, known as time dilation, means that time can flow at different rates depending on the strength of the gravitational field. For example, a clock positioned at the top of a mountain, farther from Earth's center of gravity, will tick slightly faster than one at sea level. Similarly, time moves more slowly near massive objects like black holes, where gravitational forces are immense.

This realization challenges our everyday experience of time. If time can be altered by gravity, it suggests that time is a malleable dimension, one that can be shaped and stretched like the other dimensions of space. In this sense, time is not an absolute; it is relative, dependent on the conditions of the surrounding environment. This discovery has profound implications, hinting at the possibility that time may be part of a larger, multidimensional structure that we have only begun to comprehend.

The Relativity of Time: How We Perceive the Passage of Moments

While Einstein's theories reveal time as a dimension subject to gravitational forces, our personal experience of time is shaped by a myriad of factors. The perception of time varies from one individual to another and can even change from one moment to the next. Time flies when we are engrossed in a task, yet it seems to drag during moments of boredom or anticipation. This subjective experience of time is influenced by psychological, physiological, and environmental factors, reminding us that time, as we perceive it, is not a constant.

At the biological level, our brains regulate the perception of time through a complex interplay of neurons and chemicals. For instance, adrenaline, often released during moments of excitement or fear, can cause time to appear to slow down, allowing us to process more information in a brief span. Similarly, repetitive tasks can create a sense of time compression, where hours seem to pass in the blink of an eye.

Culturally, our perception of time is shaped by the rhythms of our daily lives, whether dictated by the sun, the clock, or our own habits. In some cultures, time is perceived as a linear sequence of events, while others view it as cyclical, with past, present, and future existing in a continuous loop. This diversity of perspectives on time reflects its fundamental role in human life, as well as the mysteries that remain hidden within this dimension.

Time Travel: A Theoretical Journey Through Time

One of the most captivating ideas to emerge from modern physics is the concept of time travel. While often relegated to the realm of science fiction, time travel has a basis in the laws of physics. According to Einstein's theory of special relativity, as an object approaches the speed of light, time for that object slows down relative to an outside observer. This effect, known as time dilation, has been observed in experiments involving high-speed particles, which experience time at a different rate than slower-moving particles.

For example, astronauts traveling at near-light speed would age more slowly than people on Earth. Upon returning, they would find that more time has passed on Earth than they experienced, effectively allowing them to travel into the future. This phenomenon, while seemingly fantastical, has been confirmed by experiments with atomic clocks on high-speed aircraft, which show measurable differences in time passage compared to stationary clocks on the ground.

But what about traveling backward in time? While theoretical physics has proposed mechanisms such as wormholes—hypothetical tunnels through spacetime—there is no experimental evidence to support the feasibility of time travel to the past. Wormholes remain speculative, and the paradoxes associated with backward time travel, such as the "grandfather paradox," suggest that such journeys might be impossible or, at the very least, fraught with complexities beyond our current understanding.

The Arrow of Time: Why Does Time Move Forward?

One of the great mysteries of time is its unidirectional nature, often referred to as the "arrow of time." In our everyday experience, time flows inexorably from the past to the present to the future, and this progression appears to be irreversible. But why does time move in this direction, and could it be possible for time to flow backward?

The answer lies in the concept of entropy, which measures the degree of disorder within a system. According to the second law of thermodynamics, entropy in a closed system tends to increase over time, leading to a state of greater disorder. This principle gives time its arrow, as it dictates those certain processes—such as the breaking of a glass or the melting of ice—are irreversible. Once disorder increases, it cannot spontaneously revert to order.

However, at the quantum level, the arrow of time becomes less certain. In certain interpretations of quantum mechanics, time is reversible, and particles can exist in superpositions of states that allow for backward as well as forward progression. These phenomena challenge our classical understanding of time and suggest that, at the fundamental level, time may not behave as linearly as it appears.

Time and Multidimensional Reality: Beyond the Fourth Dimension

If time is a dimension like space, could there be other dimensions that influence it? Some theories in modern physics, such as string theory, propose the existence of additional spatial dimensions beyond the three we perceive. In these models, time is just one of several dimensions that make up the fabric of reality, and these extra dimensions could hold the key to understanding the true nature of time.

In some models of the multiverse, time may operate differently in parallel realities, with different laws governing its flow and behaviour. Imagine a universe where time flows in reverse, or one where time is circular, looping back on itself in an eternal cycle. While these ideas remain speculative, they challenge our understanding of time and open up new possibilities for exploring its hidden dimensions.

These extra dimensions also offer potential explanations for phenomena that remain unexplained by current theories. Dark matter and dark energy, which make up the majority of the universe's mass and energy, could exist in dimensions that are inaccessible to us, influencing the behaviour of time and space in ways we cannot directly observe. If these hidden dimensions interact with time, they could reveal new insights into the structure of reality and the nature of existence.

The Illusion of Time: Is Time Real?

One of the most profound questions surrounding time is whether it is a fundamental property of the universe or simply an illusion created by our perception. Some physicists argue that time is not a fundamental aspect of reality but an emergent phenomenon that arises from the interactions of particles and forces. In this view, time does not exist independently of the events that occur within it; rather, it is a by-product of change.

This perspective challenges the idea of time as a linear, continuous flow, suggesting that it may instead be composed of discrete moments, much like frames in a film. Just as the illusion of motion is created by rapidly displaying a series of still images, the perception of time may be a consequence of our minds piecing together a sequence of events. If time is an illusion, it raises fundamental questions about the nature of reality and our place within it.

Conclusion: The Hidden Dimension of Time

Time is a dimension that we cannot escape, yet it remains one of the most enigmatic aspects of existence. From the fabric of spacetime to the subjective experience of time's passage, we are constantly confronted with the mystery of time's nature and the limits of our understanding. Whether time is an illusion, a fundamental dimension, or a doorway to other realities, it challenges our perception and forces us to question the nature of reality itself.

In the end, time is a reminder that there are hidden dimensions to our existence, realms that lie beyond our perception and comprehension. As we continue to explore the mysteries of time, we may find that it holds the key to understanding the deepest questions about the universe and our place within it.

"Time is the one dimension we cannot escape. It is the thread that weaves through every moment of existence, yet its true nature remains elusive. From the ticking of a clock to the lifespan of stars, time reveals itself in ways that challenge our understanding of reality."

Chapter 14: Technology as an Extension of Perception

"Human senses are limited, but technology extends our reach beyond the boundaries of biology, allowing us to see the unseen, hear the unheard, and explore dimensions that lie beyond our natural perception. In this way, technology is not just a tool—it is an extension of what we can become."

Since the dawn of humanity, we have used tools to extend our physical capabilities, from sharpened stones to the wheel, from the plod to the printing press. Yet, in the modern era, technology has taken on a new role—not merely enhancing what we can do, but transforming how we perceive the world around us. Our biological senses, though remarkable, capture only a fraction of reality. Technology, however, can take us beyond these limits, revealing dimensions of existence that were once invisible and unimaginable.

This chapter explores how technology acts as an extension of perception, allowing us to see farther, hear more acutely, and understand more deeply than our senses alone would permit. From the invention of the telescope and the microscope to the development of artificial intelligence and quantum computing, technology is reshaping our perception of the universe, challenging us to rethink what is real and what is possible.

The Evolution of Perception: From Telescopes to Quantum Detectors

Our journey into the unseen began with the creation of simple tools like the lens, which magnified objects beyond what the human eye could resolve. The telescope opened up the heavens, revealing celestial bodies and distant galaxies that were previously unknown, while the microscope brought the minute world of cells and microorganisms into focus, unveiling hidden layers of life on Earth. These early technologies expanded the boundaries of perception, enabling us to explore both the vast and the minuscule.

With each new technological leap, our understanding of reality grew. Radio telescopes allowed us to capture radio waves emitted by stars and galaxies, giving us insight into cosmic phenomena beyond the visible spectrum. X-ray machines let us peer through solid matter, revolutionizing medicine and materials science. These instruments transformed our relationship with the universe, revealing that what we perceive with our eyes is only a tiny fraction of the full electromagnetic spectrum.

Today, quantum detectors and particle accelerators take us even further into realms, where particles blink in and out of existence, defying the laws of classical physics. The Large Hadron Collider, for example, smashes particles together at near-light speeds, allowing scientists to study the fundamental forces that govern the universe. These experiments have revealed particles like the Higgs boson, which was theorized long before it was observed, demonstrating the power of technology not just to extend perception, but to confirm and deepen our understanding of reality.

The Expanding Electromagnetic Spectrum: Seeing Beyond Visible Light

Humans see only a narrow band of light, known as the visible spectrum, yet this is but a tiny portion of the electromagnetic spectrum, which ranges from low-energy radio waves to high-energy gamma rays. With the help of technology, we have learned to perceive the universe across this entire spectrum, revealing phenomena that are completely invisible to the naked eye.

Infrared cameras, for example, allow us to see heat, making it possible to visualize the thermal energy emitted by objects. This technology has applications ranging from night vision to thermal imaging in medicine and engineering. Ultraviolet light, invisible to humans but perceptible to some insects and birds, reveals patterns on flowers that guide pollinators, helping scientists understand ecological interactions in new ways.

At the high-energy end of the spectrum, X-rays and gamma rays penetrate through matter, unveiling hidden structures within objects. Gamma-ray telescopes, pointed at the cosmos, have detected the energetic emissions of supernovae and black holes, providing a glimpse into the most violent events in the universe. By extending our perception across the electromagnetic spectrum, technology has transformed our understanding of both the visible and the invisible world.

Artificial Intelligence: Extending the Mind's Perception

While much of technology's role in perception has focused on expanding our physical senses, recent advances in artificial intelligence (AI) are beginning to extend our cognitive perception. AI systems can process and analyse vast amounts of data far beyond the capacity of the human brain, allowing us to detect patterns and make predictions that would be impossible for us alone.

In astronomy, AI algorithms analyse data from telescopes, identifying patterns and anomalies that may signal new celestial objects or phenomena. In medicine, AI is used to interpret medical images, diagnose diseases, and even predict patient outcomes based on vast datasets. These systems can "see" patterns in data that human observers might miss, enhancing our ability to perceive complex systems and predict their behaviour.

As AI continues to evolve, it may unlock new dimensions of perception, allowing us to understand the universe in ways that go beyond human intuition. Imagine an AI system capable of modelling multidimensional spaces, revealing insights into the nature of reality that defy traditional logic. As these systems grow more sophisticated, they may become indispensable partners in our quest to understand the universe, extending not just our senses, but our very minds.

The Rise of Quantum Computing: A New Frontier for Perception

Quantum computing represents a dramatic leap in our ability to process information, one that could fundamentally alter our understanding of reality. Unlike classical computers, which process information in binary bits (0s and 1s), quantum computers use qubits, which can exist in multiple states simultaneously thanks to the principles of superposition and entanglement. This allows quantum computers to perform calculations that are currently impossible for even the most powerful classical supercomputers.

Quantum computers have the potential to simulate complex quantum systems, providing insights into the behaviour of particles, molecules, and even the fabric of spacetime itself. For instance, they could model the behaviour of dark matter or test theories of quantum gravity, helping us probe dimensions and forces that lie beyond our current understanding.

In this sense, quantum computing is not just a technological advancement; it is a new lens through which we can perceive the universe. By harnessing the principles of quantum mechanics, we may one day be able to explore hidden dimensions, revealing aspects of reality that are inaccessible through classical means.

Virtual Reality: Blurring the Boundaries Between Physical and Virtual Worlds

Virtual reality (VR) is another technology that is transforming our perception, allowing us to step into simulated environments that are as vivid and immersive as the physical world. With VR, we can explore virtual spaces that replicate real-world locations, or even enter fantastical realms that defy the laws of physics. This technology offers a new way to experience reality, one that challenges our understanding of presence, space, and consciousness.

As VR technology advances, it may become possible to create virtual worlds that are indistinguishable from reality. This raises profound questions about the nature of perception and what it means to experience something as "real." If a virtual world can replicate the sights, sounds, and sensations of the physical world, does that make it real? And if we spend more time in virtual spaces than physical ones, how will this affect our understanding of identity, existence, and the boundaries of reality?

The intersection of VR and AI could also lead to new forms of experience that go beyond current human capabilities. Imagine virtual worlds where AI avatars interact with us, guiding us through environments that adapt to our thoughts and emotions. These experiences could expand our perception in ways that are currently unimaginable, pushing the boundaries of what it means to be human.

Technology and the Perception of Time: Moving Beyond the Present

While technology has primarily extended our spatial perception, it also has the potential to reshape our experience of time. Advances in virtual reality, artificial intelligence, and quantum computing could one day allow us to explore temporal dimensions beyond the linear progression of past, present, and future. Imagine a future where we can revisit past experiences or project ourselves into potential futures, exploring time as a dimension as malleable as space.

In a sense, technology is already altering our perception of time. Social media and instant communication tools have created a world where events happen in real-time, compressing our sense of the present and blurring the boundaries between past and future. As technology continues to evolve, it may enable us to experience time in entirely new ways, allowing us to step outside the flow of linear time and explore alternate temporal dimensions.

The Philosophical Implications: Redefining Reality Through Technology

As technology extends our perception, it forces us to confront profound philosophical questions about the nature of reality. If our understanding of the world is limited by our senses, then technology is reshaping that understanding, revealing dimensions of existence that were previously beyond our reach. But what does it mean to live in a world where reality is constantly redefined by technological advancements?

One possibility is that reality is not a fixed entity, but a construct shaped by our perception. If technology can alter our perception, then it can also alter our reality, creating a world that is fluid, dynamic, and constantly evolving. In this sense, technology is not just an extension of perception—it is a force that reshapes the very fabric of existence.

This raises questions about the future of human experience. As we continue to develop technologies that expand our perception, we may find ourselves living in a world where the boundaries between physical and virtual, real and artificial, are increasingly blurred.

In such a world, the nature of identity, consciousness, and reality itself may be fundamentally transformed.

Conclusion: The Infinite Possibilities of Perception

Technology has always been more than just a tool—it is an extension of our perception, a way for us to explore the unseen and the unknown.

From telescopes that peer into the depths of space to quantum computers that probe the fabric of reality, technology has allowed us to transcend the limitations of our senses and push the boundaries of what we can know.

As we continue to develop new technologies, we may unlock the mysteries of hidden dimensions, revealing forces that lie beyond our perception.

In this sense, technology is not just a way to see more of the world—it is a way to reshape our understanding of reality itself. The future of perception holds the promise of infinite possibility, as technology continues to expand our reach and deepen our understanding of the universe.

"Human senses are limited, but technology extends our reach beyond the boundaries of biology, allowing us to see the unseen, hear the unheard, and explore dimensions that lie beyond our natural perception. In this way, technology is not just a tool—it is an extension of what we can become."

Chapter 15: Beyond the Horizon: The Future of Perception and Reality

"As we push the boundaries of perception, we are confronted with the possibility that reality is far greater and more complex than we can imagine. The future holds the promise of new discoveries that will challenge our understanding of the universe, opening doors to dimensions and forces yet unseen."

Our journey through the unseen realms of existence has revealed a universe that is as mysterious as it is vast. From the microcosmic intricacies of bacteria to the immense and distant cosmic web, we've come to understand that what we perceive is only a fraction of what truly exists. Yet, as technology advances and our understanding of science deepens, the horizon of perception continues to expand. Each new discovery brings us closer to unravelling the mysteries of reality and, in the process, reshapes our view of the universe and our place within it.

In this final chapter, we look ahead to the future of perception. We explore the potential of multidimensional realities, the possibilities of consciousness extending beyond the physical, and the profound philosophical questions that arise when we consider that what we know may only be the beginning.

The Uncharted Territory of Parallel Realities

One of the most intriguing and speculative ideas in modern science is the concept of parallel realities. What if our universe is just one of many, existing within a vast multiverse? If parallel realities exist, they could fundamentally alter our understanding of existence. These universes might obey different physical laws, possess unique dimensions, or harbor life forms beyond anything we can imagine.

Scientists and philosophers have long speculated about the existence of these alternate realms. The multiverse hypothesis, supported by certain interpretations of quantum mechanics and string theory, suggests that countless other universes might coexist with ours. These parallel worlds could be as real as our own, yet remain inaccessible and imperceptible to us. If true, this would mean that our universe is just one small part of a much grander, multidimensional tapestry.

The pursuit of knowledge about parallel realities forces us to confront profound questions about the nature of existence. Are these other realities fundamentally connected to ours, or do they exist independently, with no influence on our own? Could our consciousness, in some way, bridge the gap between these parallel worlds, enabling us to perceive multiple dimensions of reality simultaneously? These questions push the boundaries of our understanding and challenge the limits of what we consider to be possible.

Virtual Realities: A Gateway to New Experiences

While parallel realities remain speculative, the rise of virtual reality (VR) offers a more immediate glimpse into how technology can reshape our perception of existence. VR allows us to create and inhabit digital worlds that mimic, or even surpass, the complexity of the physical universe. In virtual environments, we can explore spaces that defy the laws of physics, interact with digital beings, and experience events that would be impossible in the real world.

As VR technology evolves, it may become increasingly difficult to distinguish between virtual and physical experiences. Advanced simulations could replicate sensory experiences with such precision that they become indistinguishable from reality. In this sense, VR could act as a bridge to other forms of existence, allowing us to experience alternate realities and perhaps even glimpse dimensions that are otherwise inaccessible.

The implications of VR extend beyond entertainment and into the realms of philosophy and psychology. If virtual experiences can feel as real as physical ones, what does that mean for our understanding of reality? Could we one day choose to live in virtual worlds, abandoning the physical for the digital? And if so, what would that mean for our sense of self, identity, and existence? As VR blurs the boundaries between the real and the artificial, we may find ourselves questioning the very nature of reality.

The Role of Consciousness: Beyond the Physical

As we explore the limits of perception, we must also consider the role of consciousness—the subjective experience of being aware and observing the world. While science has made significant strides in understanding the brain, consciousness remains one of the most profound mysteries of existence. What is consciousness, and how does it relate to the physical world? Could it be that our awareness is not confined to our bodies, but rather, part of a larger, interconnected field of existence?

Some theories suggest that consciousness is a fundamental aspect of the universe, woven into the very fabric of reality. This view, often referred to as panpsychism, posits that all matter possesses a form of consciousness, from the smallest particle to the largest galaxy. If true, this would mean that the universe is alive, teeming with awareness at every level of existence.

The idea that consciousness could extend beyond the physical world raises profound questions about the nature of reality. Could our minds have the ability to perceive dimensions that are hidden from our senses? Could consciousness exist independently of the body, allowing us to explore realms beyond the physical? These questions challenge our understanding of what it means to be alive and suggest that there may be layers of reality that are accessible only through the mind.

Time Perception and the Flow of Reality

As we delve into the future of perception, it becomes clear that our experience of time is also limited by our biological constraints. We perceive time as a linear progression from past to present to future, but what if this is only one way of experiencing it? Could there be other ways of perceiving time, hidden from our senses but accessible through technology or altered states of consciousness?

Some scientists and philosophers argue that time may be an illusion, a construct of the human mind that helps us make sense of the world. In this view, past, present, and future are not separate entities but rather, different aspects of a single, unified reality. If this is true, then it may be possible to experience time in ways that go beyond our current understanding.

Imagine a future where we can revisit past events, explore alternate timelines, or even perceive multiple moments simultaneously. Such experiences would challenge our understanding of causality, sequence, and change, and suggest that time itself is a dimension as flexible and dynamic as space. As we continue to push the boundaries of perception, we may discover that our experience of time is just one of many possible ways of interacting with reality.

The Search for Truth in a Complex Universe

The quest to understand reality is ultimately a search for truth, an attempt to make sense of a universe that is as complex as it is mysterious. Yet, as we explore the limits of perception, we must confront the possibility that reality is far greater and more intricate than we can ever fully comprehend. There will always be aspects of existence that lie beyond our reach, dimensions that are hidden from view, and forces that are invisible to our senses.

This realization forces us to adopt a stance of humility in the face of the unknown. No matter how far we extend our perception, there will always be more to discover, more mysteries to unravel. In this sense, the journey of perception is an infinite quest, a never-ending exploration of the unknown. It is a reminder that we are but a small part of a vast and complex universe, and that our understanding of reality is limited by the constraints of our senses and the boundaries of our knowledge.

Embracing the Unknown: The Future of Human Potential

As we look to the future, we must embrace the unknown, recognizing that there is always more to learn, more to explore, and more to understand. Our perception of reality is constantly evolving, shaped by new discoveries, technological advancements, and shifts in consciousness. The future holds the promise of infinite possibility, as we continue to push the boundaries of what we can know and experience.

Whether through the exploration of parallel realities, the development of virtual worlds, or the discovery of new dimensions, the future of perception is a journey into the unknown. It is an invitation to expand our understanding, to explore the limits of human potential, and to embrace the mysteries of existence. In this sense, the journey of perception is not just a quest for knowledge—it is a quest for meaning, a search for our place within the vast and ever-changing tapestry of reality.

As we continue to explore the hidden dimensions of existence, we may find that the true nature of reality is far more complex and wondrous than we can imagine. The journey is endless, the possibilities infinite, and the potential for discovery boundless. And as we venture into the unknown, we are reminded that the universe is a place of infinite wonder, filled with mysteries that are waiting to be discovered.

"As we push the boundaries of perception, we are confronted with the possibility that reality is far greater and more complex than we can imagine. The future holds the promise of new discoveries that will challenge our understanding of the universe, opening doors to dimensions and forces yet unseen."

Chapter 16: Fractals of Nature: Repeating Patterns in the Universe

"The same patterns repeat across the smallest and largest scales, revealing an underlying order that connects all of existence. From the veins in a leaf to the spiral arms of a galaxy, fractals are nature's way of showing us that everything is interconnected."

When we look around us, we may think that the world is made up of separate, distinct parts. Trees stand apart from rivers, mountains rise away from the valleys, and the stars hang far above the earth. But on closer inspection, it becomes evident that a hidden structure runs through all things—a web of interconnected patterns that repeats at every level of reality. These are fractals: endlessly self-similar structures that are as beautiful as they are complex.

This chapter delves into the fascinating world of fractals, those mesmerizing forms that echo through nature, mathematics, and even human consciousness. More than just abstract patterns, fractals offer a glimpse into the fundamental workings of the universe, showing us that reality may be far more connected and unified than it appears.

Fractals in Mathematics: The Infinite Within the Finite

Fractals first emerged as a mathematical concept in the late 19th century, when mathematicians like Georg Cantor and Henri Poincaré began exploring non-linear systems and infinite sets. But it wasn't until the late 20th century, with the advent of computers, that the true depth of fractals was unveiled. Benoît Mandelbrot, often credited as the father of fractal geometry, introduced the idea that these shapes could be used to describe complex, irregular forms in nature that traditional Euclidean geometry could not capture.

Mathematically, fractals are shapes that exhibit self-similarity across different scales, meaning that each part of a fractal is a miniature, but exact or approximate, copy of the whole. The Mandelbrot set, perhaps the most famous fractal, is generated by a simple mathematical equation. When visualized, it produces an endlessly intricate pattern, with infinite detail that can be zoomed into forever, revealing ever more complex and beautiful forms.

But fractals are not just about abstract beauty; they embody the concept of infinite complexity within finite bounds. This paradoxical property suggests that even within the limited boundaries of a natural object, such as a coastline or a tree, an infinite amount of information can be encoded. This hints at a universe that is both finite in form and infinite in detail—a universe that, like a fractal, holds mysteries within mysteries.

The Language of Nature: Fractals All Around Us

Fractals are not merely mathematical curiosities; they are deeply embedded in the very fabric of nature. One of the most captivating aspects of fractals is their ubiquity. No matter where we look, from the branching of rivers to the formations of clouds, fractals reveal themselves. This self-similarity hints at an underlying unity in the natural world, a common thread that runs through the complexity and chaos of life.

Consider the branching patterns found in trees, blood vessels, and lightning. Each branch splits off into smaller branches, which themselves split off into even smaller ones, mimicking the larger structure. This recursive process, repeated across countless scales, is the essence of fractal geometry. It allows for maximum surface area within a limited space—a feature that is vital for processes like nutrient absorption in plants and oxygen exchange in the human lungs.

Even the jagged, seemingly chaotic lines of a mountain range or a coastline follow fractal patterns. The roughness of a coastline appears unchanged whether you look at it from an airplane or walk along the shore. This phenomenon, known as scale invariance, illustrates how fractals capture the essence of nature's complexity, regardless of the scale of observation.

In fact, many natural systems utilize fractal principles to optimize their functions. Trees, for example, maximize their exposure to sunlight by arranging their branches in fractal patterns. Blood vessels distribute nutrients and oxygen efficiently by branching fractally throughout the body. These structures are not random; they are highly organized and optimized, shaped by the same underlying principles that govern the cosmos.

Fractals in the Cosmos: Patterns Across Space and Time

The principles of fractal geometry extend far beyond the Earth, reaching out into the cosmos itself. Astronomers have observed that galaxies, much like the trees and rivers on our planet, exhibit fractal-like structures. The spiral arms of galaxies mimic the same logarithmic spirals found in seashells and hurricanes, suggesting that fractal patterns are not limited to Earth but may be a universal blueprint.

On an even grander scale, the cosmic web—the vast network of filaments that connect galaxies and galaxy clusters—reveals a fractal structure. This web, made up of dark matter and regular matter, stretches across the observable universe, forming a pattern of nodes and filaments that resembles a colossal spider's web. The structure is eerily similar to the neural networks found in the human brain, hinting at a fractal organization that pervades all levels of existence.

These cosmic fractals raise profound questions about the nature of the universe. Are these patterns a coincidence, or do they suggest that the universe itself operates on fractal principles? Could it be that the same laws govern the smallest subatomic particles and the largest structures in the cosmos, and that these laws manifest as fractal patterns?

Fractals as a Window into Chaos and Order

Fractals occupy a unique space between chaos and order. They are born from simple equations, yet they produce infinitely complex structures. This duality makes fractals a powerful metaphor for understanding the balance between stability and unpredictability in the universe.

In chaotic systems, fractals help us make sense of seemingly random events. The behaviour of weather patterns, stock market fluctuations, and even population dynamics can be described using fractal geometry. These systems may appear chaotic on the surface, but fractals reveal an underlying order, a self-similar structure that persists amid the chaos.

The study of fractals has even led to the development of chaos theory, which seeks to understand complex systems that are sensitive to initial conditions. A small change in a fractal equation can produce dramatically different results, a phenomenon famously illustrated by the "butterfly effect." This sensitivity to initial conditions is a defining feature of chaotic systems, and fractals provide the mathematical framework for exploring it.

Fractals in Art, Music, and Human Consciousness

The influence of fractals extends beyond science and nature, permeating art, music, and even the human mind. Fractal patterns have been used in art for centuries, long before they were formally defined. From the intricate designs of Islamic architecture to the swirling motifs of Van Gogh's paintings, artists have instinctively recognized and replicated fractal patterns.

In music, fractal structures can be found in the compositions of Johann Sebastian Bach, where recursive patterns create harmony and complexity. Modern musicians have also explored fractals in electronic music, using computer algorithms to generate compositions that reflect the self-similar structure of fractals.

The human mind itself may be fractal in nature. Studies have shown that the structure of our neural networks exhibits fractal patterns, with smaller clusters of neurons mimicking the organization of larger networks. This self-similarity extends to the way we process information, as our thoughts often branch and loop back on themselves in a fractal-like manner. It is as though our very consciousness is built upon the same fractal principles that shape the universe.

The Philosophy of Fractals: A Glimpse into the Infinite

Fractals invite us to contemplate the infinite within the finite. They suggest that within every part of the universe, no matter how small, there is an endless depth of complexity waiting to be discovered. This idea challenges our traditional understanding of reality, blurring the line between the finite and the infinite, the known and the unknown.

Philosophically, fractals embody the concept of interconnectedness. They show us that every part of the universe is connected to every other part, that each leaf, river, and star is a reflection of a larger whole. This idea resonates with ancient philosophies, such as the Buddhist concept of Indra's Net, which envisions the universe as an infinite web of jewels, each reflecting all others in an endless cycle of interdependence.

Fractals remind us that we are part of a vast, interconnected cosmos, one that operates on principles that are both familiar and alien. They offer a glimpse into the mysteries of existence, suggesting that the universe is far more complex and unified than we can imagine.

"The same patterns repeat across the smallest and largest scales, revealing an underlying order that connects all of existence. From the veins in a leaf to the spiral arms of a galaxy, fractals are nature's way of showing us that everything is interconnected."

Chapter 17: The Limits of Perception: What We Cannot See or Know

"No matter how far we extend our vision—whether through telescopes aimed at distant galaxies or microscopes focused on the smallest particles—there will always be limits to what we can perceive. The boundaries of perception remind us that there is more to reality than we will ever truly know."

Throughout human history, we have pushed the boundaries of what we can perceive, extending our senses through technology and science. We have explored the furthest reaches of space and the smallest subatomic particles, revealing a universe filled with wonders and complexities. Yet, for all our advancements, we are still limited by the constraints of our senses and our instruments. No matter how far we reach, there are aspects of reality that remain beyond our grasp.

In this chapter, we examine these boundaries of perception, exploring the edges of human understanding and the mysteries that lie beyond them. From the biological limits of our senses to the vast, invisible realms of dark matter and parallel universes, the limits of perception challenge our understanding of reality and remind us that we are only beginning to scratch the surface of the unknown.

The Biological Boundaries of Human Senses

Our perception of the world is fundamentally limited by the biological constraints of our senses. Humans can see only a narrow range of the electromagnetic spectrum, known as visible light, which spans from violet to red. Beyond this narrow band lies a world of invisible radiation: ultraviolet, infrared, X-rays, gamma rays, and radio waves, all of which are inaccessible to our unaided eyes. Despite their invisibility, these forms of light are constantly interacting with our surroundings, affecting everything from the colours of the sky to the warmth of sunlight.

Similarly, our hearing is limited to a specific range of frequencies, typically between 20 Hz and 20,000 Hz. But sounds exist far beyond this range. Dogs, for example, can hear much higher frequencies, allowing them to perceive sounds that are inaudible to humans. On the other end of the spectrum, elephants can hear low-frequency infrasound, which travels long distances and is used for communication across miles.

If our senses are so limited, then what other aspects of reality might we be missing? The colours of ultraviolet light reveal patterns on flowers that are invisible to us, yet perfectly visible to bees, who rely on these patterns to find nectar. Snakes can detect infrared radiation, allowing them to see the heat signatures of their prey. Each of these creatures experiences a different world, one shaped by senses that extend far beyond our own.

What if we, too, are surrounded by unseen worlds—realities that are invisible simply because we lack the biological equipment to perceive them? These hidden realms remind us that our experience of the world is only a sliver of what truly exists.

The Quantum Realm: A World Beyond Intuition

One of the most perplexing and elusive areas of reality lies within the quantum realm, a world governed by rules that defy our everyday experience. In the quantum world, particles like electrons and photons behave in ways that are completely counterintuitive. They can exist in multiple places at once, pass through barriers they should not be able to penetrate, and even affect each other instantaneously across vast distances—a phenomenon known as quantum entanglement.

The famous double-slit experiment illustrates the strangeness of the quantum world. When particles of light, or photons, are shot at a barrier with two slits, they behave like waves, creating an interference pattern on the other side. But if we try to observe which slit a photon passes through, it behaves like a particle instead, and the interference pattern disappears. This suggests that the mere act of observation affects the outcome, as if reality itself depends on whether or not we are watching.

Quantum mechanics challenges our basic understanding of reality. In this world, particles do not have definite positions or velocities until they are measured; instead, they exist as a probability cloud of potential outcomes.

This indeterminate state defies our classical understanding of cause and effect, leaving us to wonder whether the quantum realm operates according to principles that are fundamentally beyond our perception.

If the quantum world is truly beyond our intuitive grasp, then what other realities might exist that we cannot even begin to comprehend? The quantum realm offers a tantalizing glimpse into the limits of human understanding, reminding us that reality is far stranger than we can imagine.

Dark Matter and Dark Energy: The Unseen Universe

One of the greatest mysteries of modern science is the existence of dark matter and dark energy, which together make up about 95% of the universe's total mass and energy. Unlike ordinary matter, dark matter does not emit, absorb, or reflect light, making it completely invisible to all forms of electromagnetic radiation. We cannot see it, feel it, or interact with it directly, yet its gravitational effects on visible matter are undeniable.

Dark matter is thought to be the glue that holds galaxies together. Without it, galaxies would fly apart under their own rotational speeds. Despite its pervasive influence, dark matter remains elusive. Scientists have not yet identified what it is made of, and its existence raises profound questions about the nature of reality.

Then there is dark energy, an even more mysterious force that appears to be driving the accelerated expansion of the universe. Unlike gravity, which pulls objects together, dark energy seems to have a repulsive effect, pushing galaxies away from each other at an ever-increasing rate. We have no way of perceiving dark energy directly, and its nature remains one of the biggest enigmas in cosmology.

The existence of dark matter and dark energy reminds us that the universe is full of unseen forces, shaping the cosmos in ways that are beyond our perception. If we cannot detect the majority of the universe, then how much do we truly know about reality? The unseen universe challenges our understanding, suggesting that we may be blind to the forces that shape our existence.

The Multiverse Hypothesis: Realities Beyond Our Own

Another fascinating yet speculative frontier lies in the concept of the multiverse—the idea that our universe is just one of many, each existing within a vast, multidimensional space. According to certain interpretations of quantum mechanics and string theory, these parallel universes may exist side by side, with each having its own set of physical laws, dimensions, and conditions for life.

If the multiverse exists, then our universe is only a small part of an unimaginably vast and diverse reality. Each parallel universe could have different fundamental constants, alternate histories, or even dimensions beyond the three we experience. Some might be almost identical to ours, while others could be completely alien.

The multiverse hypothesis raises profound questions about the nature of reality. If other universes exist, then what role do they play in shaping our own? Could they interact with our universe in ways that are invisible to us? The possibility of parallel worlds suggests that there may be realms of existence that we can never perceive or understand, forever hidden beyond the veil of our limited perception.

Philosophical Implications of Perceptual Boundaries

The limits of perception have deep philosophical implications. If there are forces, dimensions, or entire universes beyond what we can perceive, how can we ever claim to have a complete understanding of reality? Are we, like fish in a pond, confined to our small corner of existence, unaware of the vast ocean beyond?

Some philosophers argue that our perception of reality is not an objective truth but a construct of our senses and cognitive processes. In this view, reality is shaped by the limits of our perception, and we may be blind to aspects of existence that lie beyond our biological and technological capabilities. Just as a bat experiences the world through echolocation and a snake through infrared detection, we too are limited by the tools with which we perceive.

The idea that there may be fundamental limits to what we can know forces us to confront the possibility that reality is far more complex than we can ever imagine. It challenges the assumption that the universe can be fully understood and reminds us to remain humble in the face of the unknown.

Conclusion: Embracing the Unknown

The journey of human knowledge is a quest to push the boundaries of perception, to see beyond the horizon and explore the hidden layers of reality. Yet, for all our advancements, there will always be limits to what we can perceive. The universe is vast, and even with the most sophisticated tools, we may never fully grasp its mysteries.

But these limits are not a cause for despair; rather, they are an invitation to wonder. They remind us that we are part of a much larger, more complex reality—one that is filled with hidden forces, unseen dimensions, and possibilities beyond our wildest imagination. In embracing the unknown, we open ourselves to the infinite beauty and complexity of existence, forever expanding the horizons of what we can perceive and understand.

"No matter how far we extend our vision—whether through telescopes aimed at distant galaxies or microscopes focused on the smallest particles—there will always be limits to what we can perceive. The boundaries of perception remind us that there is more to reality than we will ever truly know."

Chapter 18: Multidimensional Realities: The Possibility of Other Dimensions

"We live in a universe of three spatial dimensions, but what if there are others—hidden dimensions that shape our reality in ways we cannot perceive? These unseen realms could hold the key to understanding the forces that govern the cosmos."

From the small to the vast, our journey through the hidden layers of existence has taken us across scales and forces that shape our universe in ways we are only beginning to understand. But what if the world as we know it is only one part of a much larger reality—one where additional dimension exists, hidden from our view and holding secrets that could redefine our understanding of space, time, and existence itself? In this chapter, we delve into the tantalizing possibility that our universe is embedded within a multidimensional cosmos, and that these hidden dimensions could unlock answers to some of the deepest mysteries of the universe.

Beyond the Three Dimensions: A Glimpse into the Fourth

For most of human history, the concept of dimensions has been confined to the three spatial dimensions we experience—length, width, and height. Our understanding of the universe is fundamentally based on these three dimensions, yet physics hints that reality may extend far beyond them.

In the early 20th century, Albert Einstein introduced the idea that time itself could be considered a fourth dimension, woven together with the three spatial dimensions to form what we now call spacetime. According to Einstein's theory of general relativity, massive objects like stars and planets warp spacetime, creating the effects we perceive as gravity. In this view, time is not a separate entity but a fluid dimension that bends and stretches in response to mass and energy.

However, the fourth dimension of time is only the beginning. Theoretical physics suggests that there could be more dimensions beyond the ones we experience, hidden from our perception yet essential to the fabric of the cosmos. If these extra dimensions exist, they could reveal new aspects of reality, connecting our universe to a much larger and more complex multiverse.

String Theory and the Hidden Dimensions of the Universe

One of the most compelling theories that suggest the existence of extra dimensions is string theory. According to this theory, the fundamental building blocks of the universe are not particles like electrons or quarks but tiny, vibrating strings of energy. These strings vibrate at specific frequencies, giving rise to the particles and forces we observe. However, for these strings to exist, the universe must have more than the familiar three dimensions of space.

String theory proposes that there are at least ten dimensions—some theories even suggest eleven or more—where the additional dimensions are "curled up" so tightly that they are imperceptible to us. This concept of compactified dimensions suggests that, while we cannot see or measure these extra dimensions directly, they influence the behaviour of particles and forces in ways we are only beginning to understand.

One of the great mysteries of physics is why gravity is so much weaker than the other fundamental forces, like electromagnetism. String theory offers a possible explanation: gravity may be spreading out into these hidden dimensions, which could make it appear weaker in our three-dimensional world. If this is true, then the full strength of gravity might be revealed only in higher dimensions, a tantalizing hint that our perception of reality is incomplete.

The Fifth Dimension and Beyond: Theories of Multidimensional Reality

While string theory suggests ten or eleven dimensions, physicists and mathematicians have speculated about the existence of even higher dimensions, each with its own unique properties and potential. What would a fifth dimension look like? Could there be a sixth, seventh, or even higher dimensions beyond our comprehension?

Some theorists propose that additional dimensions could allow for shortcuts through spacetime, enabling phenomena like wormholes—hypothetical tunnels that connect distant points in space. In this view, higher dimensions might make possible forms of travel and communication that seem like science fiction in our three-dimensional world. For example, if a fifth dimension exists, it could allow for instant connections across vast distances, offering a glimpse into a universe where the limits of space and time are transcended.

Theoretical physicist Lisa Randall has proposed that the universe may contain "brane-worlds," parallel realities existing in higher dimensions that we cannot perceive. According to this theory, our universe could be a three-dimensional brane floating within a higher-dimensional space, much like a sheet of paper floating in a room. Other branes could exist alongside ours, each with its own distinct properties and inhabitants, yet completely invisible to us.

The Multiverse: Parallel Realities and Alternate Dimensions

The idea of extra dimensions also opens the door to the concept of the multiverse—a vast collection of parallel realities, each with its own laws of physics and conditions for life. According to some interpretations of quantum mechanics and string theory, our universe could be one of countless others, each existing in a different dimension and experiencing a unique version of reality.

In a multiverse, there could be worlds where gravity is stronger, where time flows backward, or where life exists in forms beyond our imagination. Each universe might be completely self-contained, with its own rules and limitations, yet interconnected in ways that we cannot perceive. Some theorists even suggest that these parallel universes could occasionally interact with ours, creating phenomena that seem inexplicable within our three-dimensional framework.

One interpretation of quantum mechanics, known as the Many-Worlds Hypothesis, suggests that every possible outcome of every event creates a new universe, resulting in a constantly branching multiverse where every possibility is realized. If this is true, then there could be a universe for every choice we have ever made, and every path we have ever taken, extending our reality into an infinite number of parallel dimensions.

Interacting with the Invisible: The Search for Evidence of Extra Dimensions

While the idea of multidimensional realities is intriguing, it remains speculative, and scientists are actively searching for ways to test these theories. One approach involves the study of particle collisions in powerful accelerators like the Large Hadron Collider (LHC). By smashing particles together at high energies, researchers hope to create conditions that could reveal the influence of extra dimensions, perhaps by detecting particles that momentarily slip into a higher dimension before reappearing in ours.

Another avenue of exploration is the study of gravitational waves, ripples in the fabric of spacetime caused by massive cosmic events like black hole collisions. Some theories suggest that gravitational waves could be affected by extra dimensions, and that their behaviour might provide clues to the existence of hidden realms. Researchers are also exploring the possibility that dark matter—a mysterious form of matter that makes up much of the universe—could be interacting with higher dimensions, creating effects that we can observe but not fully explain.

These experiments are still in their early stages, and the search for extra dimensions is fraught with challenges. Yet, with each new discovery, we come closer to understanding whether multidimensional realities are a true part of the universe, or simply a fascinating hypothesis.

Philosophical Implications: The Nature of Reality and Existence

The possibility of multidimensional realities raises profound philosophical questions about the nature of existence. If there are dimensions beyond our perception, then what does it mean to be a conscious being? Are we limited to experiencing only a fraction of reality, while vast realms lie beyond our reach?

Some philosophers suggest that if other dimensions exist, they might host forms of consciousness that are completely alien to us, beings that perceive and interact with reality in ways that are incomprehensible within our three-dimensional framework. This idea challenges our understanding of consciousness, identity, and what it means to be alive.

Moreover, the idea that our universe could be one of many raises' questions about the nature of individuality and the self. If there are countless versions of us living in parallel realities, then what defines our true self? Are we unique, or are we simply one iteration among infinite possibilities?

The possibility of higher dimensions also invites us to reconsider our place in the cosmos. Just as ants live in a two-dimensional world, oblivious to the complexities of our three-dimensional existence, we too may be unaware of the vast, multidimensional realms that lie beyond our perception. In this sense, the search for extra dimensions is not just a scientific quest but a philosophical journey into the nature of reality itself.

Conclusion: Embracing the Unknown Dimensions of Existence

The idea of multidimensional realities invites us to imagine a universe that is far more complex, vast, and mysterious than we can perceive. Whether through string theory, the multiverse, or the hidden dimensions of spacetime, the concept of extra dimensions challenges us to expand our understanding of what is possible and to embrace the idea that reality may extend beyond the limits of our senses and technology.

As we continue to explore the cosmos, we must remain open to the possibility that we are only seeing a small part of a much larger tapestry—a tapestry woven with dimensions and realities that transcend our perception. The search for extra dimensions is a testament to the boundless curiosity and imagination of the human spirit, a reminder that the universe is filled with mysteries yet to be discovered.

In the end, the idea of multidimensional realities invites us to wonder not only about the nature of the universe but about the nature of ourselves. Are we beings limited to a three-dimensional world, or are we part of a much larger, more complex reality? The answers may lie beyond the horizon of perception, waiting to be discovered by those willing to look beyond the visible and into the infinite.

"We live in a universe of three spatial dimensions, but what if there are others—hidden dimensions that shape our reality in ways we cannot perceive? These unseen

realms could hold the key to understanding the forces that govern the cosmos."

Chapter 19: Consciousness and the Universe

"Is the universe aware of itself? Through the lens of consciousness, we seek not just to understand existence but to ponder the awareness that shapes it. Could consciousness be the unseen force binding reality together, spanning dimensions beyond our comprehension?"

Throughout the journey of exploring the hidden aspects of reality, consciousness has remained a silent observer, guiding our curiosity. Yet consciousness itself is a profound mystery. What if consciousness isn't merely a product of the universe but a fundamental component of it—a pervasive element woven into the very fabric of existence? This idea has captivated thinkers, scientists, and philosophers for centuries. In this chapter, we delve into the connection between consciousness and the universe, contemplating theories that suggest consciousness may be as fundamental as space, time, and matter.

Panpsychism: Consciousness as a Universal Trait

One of the most intriguing theories that address the ubiquity of consciousness is **panpsychism**. Panpsychism proposes that consciousness is a fundamental aspect of all things, not just humans or animals but every atom, molecule, and subatomic particle in the universe. In this view, consciousness is a pervasive quality rather than an emergent property of complex brains.

Imagine a universe where every particle, from the smallest quark to the largest galaxy, possesses a rudimentary form of consciousness. Though these levels of awareness differ vastly from human experience, they collectively contribute to a universal field of consciousness. This concept may sound radical, but it echoes ancient philosophies and spiritual traditions that propose a connectedness in all things. Modern panpsychists, such as philosopher Philip Goff, argue that accepting consciousness as a fundamental property could provide explanations for why and how consciousness arises in complex beings like us.

Integrated Information Theory: Measuring Consciousness in the Cosmos

In our attempt to quantify consciousness, **Integrated Information Theory (IIT)** has emerged as a leading scientific approach. IIT suggests that consciousness arises from the integration of information within a system. The more complex the information integration, the greater the degree of consciousness.

According to IIT, consciousness is not exclusive to humans or animals; it could, theoretically, be found in any sufficiently complex system, potentially extending to artificial intelligence, ecosystems, and even the universe itself. Could the cosmos be one such system—

a self-aware entity composed of countless interconnected parts?

Imagine the universe as an infinitely vast network of information, woven together by its own structure and laws. Stars, planets, galaxies, and even black holes could be seen as nodes within this network, each contributing to a cosmic consciousness. The very concept of the universe as a thinking entity forces us to confront the notion that consciousness might not be limited to biological systems but could exist wherever there is sufficient complexity and interconnectivity.

Consciousness as a Multidimensional Bridge

If consciousness is indeed fundamental to the universe, it may not be confined to the three-dimensional reality we experience. Some theorists suggest that consciousness could act as a bridge between dimensions, allowing us to perceive and interact with higher levels of reality. **Multidimensional consciousness** posits that while our physical bodies are bound to three-dimensional space, our minds—or perhaps our awareness—can transcend these limitations.

Meditative practices, mystical experiences, and even psychedelic journeys have long hinted at the possibility of consciousness expanding beyond ordinary perception, reaching realms that defy our physical understanding. This is where consciousness could potentially interface with the hidden dimensions discussed earlier in this book. If consciousness can indeed bridge dimensions, it might provide us with glimpses into realities that are otherwise beyond reach.

Consider the potential implications: if consciousness can move freely across dimensions, then our thoughts, emotions, and perhaps even our awareness might exist on a plane where the constraints of time and space are irrelevant. This could explain experiences of precognition, telepathy, or other phenomena that challenge our conventional understanding of reality.

The Universe as a Conscious Entity: The Living Cosmos

Could the universe itself possess a form of awareness? This question leads us to the concept of a **living cosmos**, an idea that has found proponents among both scientists and mystics. If the universe is conscious, it might be aware of its own evolution, actively participating in the creation and transformation of its contents.

In this view, the cosmos is not a cold, mechanical entity but a living system with a purpose, evolving toward greater complexity and self-awareness. Just as neurons form networks that give rise to the human mind, galaxies and star systems could be the building blocks of a vast cosmic brain, each part contributing to a collective awareness that is the universe itself.

The idea that the universe might be conscious also resonates with **Gaia Theory**, which views Earth as a living organism, with all life forms interconnected and collectively contributing to the planet's health and stability. Extending Gaia Theory to the cosmos, one could argue that all components of the universe work together to sustain an overarching cosmic consciousness.

Quantum Mechanics and the Role of the Observer

Quantum mechanics has shown us that the observer plays a crucial role in shaping reality. The **observer effect** suggests that simply by observing a particle, we influence its state. This raises the question: Could consciousness itself be the force that shapes the universe?

Some physicists, such as John Archibald Wheeler, have suggested that the universe might be a **"participatory universe,"** wherein consciousness and matter are inextricably linked. Wheeler's famous phrase, "It from bit," implies that information (or consciousness) underpins all physical reality. This idea challenges us to consider the possibility that without consciousness, the universe as we know it might not even exist.

The Search for Cosmic Consciousness: A Journey into the Unknown

As we explore the universe, we find ourselves not only seeking to understand matter and energy but also probing the depths of consciousness itself. The quest for cosmic consciousness is ultimately a journey into the unknown, where science, philosophy, and spirituality intersect.

Could our own consciousness be a small part of a greater awareness? Perhaps as we unlock more of the universe's mysteries, we will also unlock hidden aspects of our own minds. For now, we are left with profound questions: Does the universe think? Are we, in some way, the eyes and ears of a conscious cosmos? And if so, what does that mean for our place in the grand scheme of things?

Conclusion: The Mystery of Consciousness in an Expansive Universe

As we reach the end of this chapter, we are left with more questions than answers. Consciousness remains one of the most profound and elusive aspects of reality, a force that might be as integral to the universe as space and time. Whether it is a product of our brains, a fundamental property of all matter, or a bridge to other dimensions, consciousness continues to beckon us to explore its depths.

As we continue our journey through the cosmos, we are reminded that we are not just observers of the universe but participants in its ongoing story. Consciousness might be the very essence of what it means to be a part of the universe—a universe that may, in some mysterious way, be aware of itself through us.

"Is the universe aware of itself? Through the lens of consciousness, we seek not just to understand existence but to ponder the awareness that shapes it. Could consciousness be the unseen force binding reality together, spanning dimensions beyond our comprehension?"

Chapter 20: The Symphony of Existence: Harmonizing Science, Philosophy, and Spirituality

"In seeking to understand the mysteries of existence, we often turn to science, philosophy, or spirituality. But what if, rather than separate paths, these are all parts of a grand symphony—different melodies, harmonizing to reveal the profound truths of reality?"

In our quest to understand the universe, we typically look to science for answers, to philosophy for meaning, and to spirituality for purpose. These disciplines are often seen as distinct paths, each with its own set of principles, practices, and perspectives. However, as we've explored the cosmos, consciousness, and the unseen dimensions of reality, a unifying thread has emerged—one that suggests these disciplines are not so separate after all. Rather, they might be facets of a single, harmonious symphony, each adding its own notes to the melody of existence.

In this final chapter, we explore the convergence of science, philosophy, and spirituality, contemplating how their interconnectedness may offer a more profound understanding of the cosmos and our place within it.

Science: The Language of the Universe

Science is often regarded as the most concrete and empirical means of understanding reality. Through observation, experimentation, and the rigorous application of logic, science has uncovered many of the laws that govern the physical world. From the behaviour of subatomic particles to the movement of galaxies, science provides us with a framework to explore the mechanisms of existence.

Yet, even as science unravels the mysteries of the universe, it often leads to more questions than answers. The pursuit of knowledge has taken us to the edges of the observable cosmos and into the paradoxes of quantum mechanics, revealing realms where conventional logic breaks down. Here, at the boundaries of scientific understanding, we begin to see that science alone may not be sufficient to capture the full essence of reality.

It is here, at the very edges of knowledge, that science reaches out to other modes of understanding—namely, philosophy and spirituality. Where science seeks to answer *how* things work, it leaves space for philosophy to ask *why* and for spirituality to explore *what it means*.

Philosophy: The Quest for Meaning

If science provides the language to describe the universe, then philosophy offers the context to ponder it. Philosophy has long grappled with the big questions— What is the nature of reality? What does it mean to exist? Why are we here? These questions extend beyond the realm of testable hypotheses and observable data, inviting us to explore the deeper implications of what we know.

In considering the nature of time, consciousness, and multidimensional realities, we find ourselves inevitably drawn into philosophical inquiry. The great philosophers, from Plato to Descartes, have wrestled with questions that remain relevant even as science has advanced. Today, philosophy continues to serve as a bridge, connecting the tangible discoveries of science with the abstract realms of meaning and purpose.

One of the most significant contributions of philosophy to our understanding of the cosmos is its emphasis on interconnectedness. While science often breaks down the universe into its constituent parts, philosophy encourages us to see the whole. It suggests that the universe may be more than the sum of its parts, a vast, interconnected web where each piece influences the other. This perspective aligns closely with many spiritual traditions, which also emphasize the unity of all things.

Spirituality: The Pursuit of Purpose

While science and philosophy provide tools for understanding and meaning, spirituality offers a path toward purpose. Spirituality goes beyond intellectual exploration, engaging our emotions, intuition, and personal experiences. It invites us to consider the possibility that there is a deeper purpose to existence, one that transcends the physical and material world.

Spirituality encompasses a wide range of beliefs and practices, but at its core, it often seeks to connect us with something greater than ourselves. This might be a divine presence, a universal consciousness, or a sense of oneness with the cosmos. Through practices like meditation, prayer, and contemplation, spirituality opens up pathways for personal transformation, allowing us to engage with the mysteries of existence in a profoundly personal way.

In exploring the concepts of consciousness, multidimensional realities, and the unseen architecture of the universe, we find that spirituality and science are not as far apart as they may seem. Quantum mechanics, for example, has led some scientists to explore ideas that resonate with spiritual concepts, such as the interconnectedness of all things or the possibility of a universal consciousness. These intersections suggest that spirituality may provide valuable insights into the aspects of reality that science has yet to fully explain.

The Convergence of Science, Philosophy, and Spirituality

As we reach the culmination of our exploration, it becomes clear that science, philosophy, and spirituality are not isolated disciplines but are deeply interconnected. Each offers a unique perspective on reality, and together, they provide a richer, more nuanced understanding of existence.

Consider the concept of **panpsychism**, which proposes that consciousness is a fundamental aspect of the universe. This idea bridges the gap between science, which studies the physical world, and spirituality, which seeks to understand consciousness and purpose. Similarly, **quantum mechanics** challenges our notions of reality, prompting philosophical questions about the nature of existence and hinting at spiritual ideas of interconnectedness and unity.

In this way, science, philosophy, and spirituality converge to create a more complete picture of the universe. Like different instruments in an orchestra, each discipline plays its part, harmonizing to reveal a symphony of existence that is greater than the sum of its parts.

Embracing the Mystery: The Role of Wonder

One of the most beautiful aspects of this convergence is the sense of wonder it inspires. Science, philosophy, and spirituality each cultivate a sense of awe, reminding us that the universe is vast, complex, and deeply mysterious. While science provides us with knowledge, philosophy offers wisdom, and spirituality fosters a sense of connection. Together, they invite us to embrace the mystery, to approach the universe not just as observers, but as participants in a cosmic dance.

This sense of wonder is crucial because it encourages humility and openness, qualities that are essential for exploring the unknown. In recognizing that we do not have all the answers, we remain receptive to new ideas and experiences, allowing ourselves to be transformed by the journey of discovery. As we stand on the threshold of knowledge, we are reminded that the universe is far greater than our limited understanding, and that is precisely what makes it so beautiful.

Conclusion: The Symphony of Existence

As we conclude this chapter and our exploration of *Spectrums Unseen*, we are left with a profound appreciation for the interconnectedness of science, philosophy, and spirituality. Together, they form a symphony of existence, each contributing to a melody that resonates with our deepest questions and aspirations. In harmonizing these different modes of thought, we gain a fuller understanding of the cosmos and our place within it.

This journey has taken us to the edges of perception, beyond the boundaries of the visible, and into the realms of consciousness and multidimensional realities. Along the way, we have seen that science, philosophy, and spirituality are not separate paths but different notes in the same grand composition. As we continue to explore the mysteries of existence, let us carry this harmony with us, embracing the symphony of existence and the infinite possibilities it holds.

"In seeking to understand the mysteries of existence, we often turn to science, philosophy, or spirituality. But what if, rather than separate paths, these are all parts of a grand symphony—different melodies, harmonizing to reveal the profound truths of reality?"

Chapter 21: The Infinite Journey: Embracing the Unseen Realms of Reality

"The quest for knowledge is an infinite journey, one that stretches beyond the horizons of perception and delves into the unseen realms of existence. As we reach new heights, we find that every answer uncovers deeper mysteries, inviting us to venture further into the cosmos."

We have travelled through many layers of reality, from the microscopic to the cosmic, exploring the worlds hidden within and beyond our perception. Along the way, we've encountered concepts that stretch our understanding, like multidimensional realities, quantum mechanics, and the hidden forces that govern the universe. Now, as we draw this journey to a close, we recognize that this is not the end, but rather a stepping stone on a path that stretches into the infinite.

In this final chapter, we reflect on the nature of this infinite journey—the unending quest to understand the cosmos, the mysteries we may never fully unravel, and the significance of embracing the unknown. The more we discover, the more we realize there are realms of reality that will forever remain beyond our grasp. And yet, this is precisely what makes the pursuit so profoundly meaningful.

The Unending Quest for Knowledge: A Journey Without a Destination

Human beings have always been driven by a thirst for knowledge, a desire to understand the world and our place within it. From ancient philosophers pondering the nature of existence to modern scientists probing the depths of space, we are explorers at heart, forever seeking answers to questions that seem to multiply as we go.

In many ways, the quest for knowledge is akin to an endless journey without a fixed destination. Each discovery serves as a marker along the way, revealing new vistas and opening up new questions. The more we learn, the more we realize how much we don't know, and this realization propels us to venture further, to push beyond the boundaries of what is familiar and into the unknown.

This infinite journey is not a straight path but a winding road with countless branches, each leading to new realms of understanding. For every question answered, ten more arise, reminding us that knowledge is not a finite resource, but an ever-expanding universe in its own right. The more we explore, the more we realize that there will always be uncharted territories, new dimensions to uncover, and mysteries to ponder.

The Mystery of the Unseen: A Universe Beyond Perception

Throughout this book, we have delved into the unseen realms of reality, from the hidden worlds of bacteria and cosmic waves to the mysterious nature of dark matter and extra dimensions. These unseen realms challenge our understanding of what it means to perceive, to know, and to exist. They remind us that our perception is limited, confined to a narrow band of reality that we are capable of experiencing.

Yet, it is precisely these unseen realms that fuel our curiosity. The idea that there are entire dimensions, forces, and entities that lie beyond our perception is both humbling and inspiring. It suggests that the universe is far more complex and layered than we can ever fully comprehend, and that there are aspects of reality that will forever remain shrouded in mystery.

As we reach the limits of our perception, we find that the unseen is not something to be feared, but something to be embraced. It is a reminder that there is always more to learn, more to discover, and more to experience. By embracing the unknown, we open ourselves to the possibility of new insights, new connections, and new ways of understanding the universe.

Embracing the Infinite: The Role of Wonder and Awe

In our exploration of the cosmos and the hidden dimensions of reality, we are often struck by a profound sense of wonder. This sense of awe is a powerful force, one that drives us to keep exploring, to keep asking questions, and to keep pushing the boundaries of what we know. Wonder is not just a passive experience; it is an active engagement with the mysteries of existence, a way of reaching beyond our limitations and connecting with the vastness of the universe.

Wonder and awe remind us that we are part of something much larger than ourselves, something that transcends our individual lives and connects us to the cosmos. They encourage us to look beyond the mundane, to see the beauty and complexity of the world around us, and to appreciate the infinite possibilities that lie before us. In this way, wonder becomes a guiding light, illuminating the path of our infinite journey and inspiring us to continue exploring, even when the destination is uncertain.

The Infinite Possibilities of Multidimensional Realities

As we reflect on the journey we have taken, we find that the concept of multidimensional realities serves as a fitting metaphor for the infinite journey of knowledge. Just as there are dimensions beyond our perception, there are layers of understanding that remain hidden, waiting to be uncovered. These multidimensional realities suggest that the universe is not a static place, but a dynamic and ever-changing tapestry, one that is constantly evolving and revealing new facets of itself.

The idea of multidimensional realities also challenges us to think beyond the boundaries of our current knowledge. It invites us to consider the possibility that there are realms of existence that operate according to different laws, different dimensions, and different forms of consciousness. These hidden dimensions remind us that there is always more to explore, more to learn, and more to understand.

By embracing the concept of multidimensional realities, we open ourselves to the possibility of new ways of thinking, new ways of perceiving, and new ways of experiencing the universe. We come to see that the infinite journey is not just a journey through space and time, but a journey through the many dimensions of existence, each offering its own unique insights and perspectives.

The Legacy of Exploration: Inspiring Future Generations

As we reflect on our infinite journey, we recognize that we are not the first, nor will we be the last, to seek answers to the mysteries of existence. Throughout history, countless explorers, philosophers, and scientists have contributed to the collective knowledge of humanity, paving the way for future generations to continue the quest.

Our journey is part of a larger legacy of exploration, one that stretches back to the earliest humans who looked up at the stars and wondered about their place in the cosmos. By embracing the unknown, we honour this legacy, and we pass on the torch of knowledge to those who will come after us. We inspire future generations to keep asking questions, to keep seeking answers, and to keep exploring the universe.

This legacy of exploration is not just about acquiring knowledge; it is about fostering a sense of curiosity, a love of learning, and a deep appreciation for the mysteries of existence. By nurturing these qualities in ourselves and in others, we contribute to the ongoing journey of discovery, ensuring that the quest for knowledge will continue for generations to come.

Conclusion: The Eternal Mystery of Existence

As we conclude this final chapter, we are reminded that the journey of discovery is an infinite one, with no fixed destination and no final answers. The universe is vast, complex, and filled with mysteries that will forever remain beyond our reach. Yet, it is precisely this sense of mystery that makes the journey so profoundly meaningful.

In the end, the infinite journey is not about finding answers, but about embracing the unknown, celebrating the beauty of existence, and cultivating a sense of wonder and awe. It is about recognizing that we are part of something much larger than ourselves, something that transcends our individual lives and connects us to the cosmos.

As we continue on this journey, let us carry with us the knowledge that there will always be more to discover, more to explore, and more to understand. Let us embrace the infinite possibilities that lie before us, and let us continue to seek answers to the mysteries of existence, knowing that the journey itself is the ultimate reward.

"The quest for knowledge is an infinite journey, one that stretches beyond the horizons of perception and delves into the unseen realms of existence. As we reach new heights, we find that every answer uncovers deeper mysteries, inviting us to venture further into the cosmos."

Chapter 22: The Harmony of Existence: Bridging the Seen and Unseen Worlds

"In the grand tapestry of existence, every thread, seen and unseen, is woven into a single, harmonious whole. From the smallest particle to the vastness of the cosmos, the universe speaks a language of unity and connection, inviting us to bridge the worlds we know with those that lie beyond perception."

Throughout this exploration, we have journeyed through layers of reality that encompass everything from the microscopic world of bacteria to the invisible forces of dark matter and the possibility of multidimensional realities. As we stand at the crossroads of the seen and the unseen, we find that there is a profound harmony that binds all aspects of existence together.

In this chapter, we explore the unity of existence—how the intricate web of life, space, and time converges into a cohesive, harmonious whole. We delve into the ways in which the visible and invisible realms intersect, creating a universe that is at once complex and beautifully interconnected. This chapter invites us to consider the possibility that all things, from the tiniest quark to the vast stretches of cosmic space, are part of a greater, harmonious design.

The Interconnected Web: From Quantum Particles to Cosmic Galaxies

At every scale of existence, from the infinitesimally small to the unimaginably large, we find patterns and principles that echo one another. Quantum particles, which operate at the smallest levels of reality, display a seemingly chaotic yet deeply interconnected behaviour that can influence particles across vast distances, a phenomenon known as quantum entanglement. Similarly, galaxies, which form the cosmic structure of the universe, are bound together by gravitational forces, weaving a cosmic web that connects clusters of stars and planets across unimaginable distances.

This interconnectedness suggests that the universe is not a random assembly of isolated parts, but a unified whole in which each component influences the others. The dance of galaxies and the vibrations of quantum particles are different expressions of the same underlying principles, bridging the gap between the visible and the invisible. It is as if the universe is a vast symphony, with each particle, star, and galaxy playing its part in a harmonious melody that spans all of existence.

In this symphony, every element contributes to the overall harmony, creating a universe that is both complex and deeply interconnected. This unity suggests that the distinctions we make between different scales of existence—between the micro and the macro, the physical and the metaphysical—are not as absolute as they seem. Instead, they are points along a continuum, connected by the same fundamental principles that govern all of reality.

The Role of Energy: The Universal Language

One of the most unifying forces in the universe is energy. Energy flows through all things, shaping matter, space, and time. From the light of the stars to the vibrations of sound and the pulse of electricity, energy is the common thread that ties all of existence together. It is the currency of the cosmos, a universal language that speaks to the interconnectedness of all things.

In the human body, energy manifests as electrical impulses that transmit information through the nervous system, allowing us to move, think, and feel. In the natural world, energy flows through ecosystems, cycling between plants, animals, and the environment, sustaining life in all its forms. On a cosmic scale, energy fuels the stars, powers the expansion of the universe, and shapes the very fabric of spacetime.

This continuous flow of energy is a reminder that we are part of a larger system, one in which all things are connected by the same life force. Whether we are aware of it or not, we are constantly exchanging energy with the world around us, participating in a dance that links us to the stars, the planets, and the unseen dimensions of existence. By recognizing this connection, we can begin to see ourselves as part of a larger, harmonious whole, one in which the boundaries between the self and the universe begin to dissolve.

Bridging the Gap: The Seen and Unseen Worlds in Harmony

While the visible and invisible realms may seem distinct, they are in fact deeply intertwined, each influencing the other in ways that are not always immediately apparent. The unseen forces of dark matter and dark energy, for example, shape the structure of the universe, influencing the movement of galaxies and the expansion of space itself. Though we cannot see or touch these forces, they play a crucial role in the dynamics of the visible world, creating a bridge between the known and the unknown.

Similarly, in our own lives, the intangible aspects of existence—our thoughts, emotions, and beliefs—shape our physical reality, influencing our actions, our relationships, and our experiences. Though we cannot measure or quantify these inner worlds, they are as real and as influential as the physical objects that surround us. In this way, the seen and unseen worlds exist in a state of harmony, each enriching and informing the other.

This harmony is not static but dynamic, constantly shifting and evolving as new connections are formed and old ones are transformed. It is a reminder that the universe is not a collection of separate parts, but a single, unified whole in which all things are interconnected. By bridging the gap between the visible and the invisible, we can begin to see the world in a new light, one that reveals the underlying unity of all existence.

The Balance of Forces: Order and Chaos in Harmony

At the heart of the universe is a delicate balance between order and chaos, a tension that gives rise to the complexity and beauty of existence. In the visible world, we see this balance in the intricate patterns of nature, from the branching of trees to the spiralling of galaxies. In the invisible world, we find it in the unpredictable behaviour of quantum particles and the mysterious forces that shape the cosmos.

Order and chaos are not opposing forces, but complementary aspects of a single reality. Order brings structure and stability, allowing life to flourish and systems to endure. Chaos, on the other hand, brings change and transformation, breaking down old structures to make way for new ones. Together, they create a dynamic equilibrium that sustains the universe, a balance that allows for both continuity and evolution.

This balance is reflected in all aspects of existence, from the cycles of life and death to the rise and fall of civilizations. It is a reminder that harmony is not about eliminating chaos or achieving perfect order, but about finding balance and embracing the ebb and flow of existence. By recognizing the role of both order and chaos, we can begin to see the beauty in the impermanence of life, the creativity that arises from uncertainty, and the interconnectedness of all things.

Embracing Unity: The Journey to Wholeness

As we reflect on the harmony of existence, we are reminded that we are not separate from the universe, but an integral part of it. The boundaries that seem to divide us from the world around us are illusions, products of our limited perception. In reality, we are connected to all things, bound together by the same forces, energies, and patterns that shape the cosmos.

This recognition invites us to embrace a sense of unity, to see ourselves as part of a larger, interconnected whole. It encourages us to cultivate a sense of empathy and compassion, not only for other human beings but for all forms of life and all aspects of existence. By embracing unity, we can begin to see the world as it truly is—a harmonious, interconnected web in which all things are connected and all beings are part of a larger, universal family.

The journey to wholeness is not about achieving a state of perfect harmony, but about recognizing the unity that already exists within and around us. It is about learning to see the world with new eyes, to appreciate the beauty of both the seen and unseen realms, and to embrace the infinite possibilities that arise from the interplay of all things. In this way, we can begin to live in harmony with the universe, to become a conscious part of the symphony of existence.

Conclusion: The Infinite Dance of Existence

As we conclude this chapter, we are reminded that the harmony of existence is not a static state, but an infinite dance that unfolds across all scales of reality. From the smallest particle to the largest galaxy, from the visible to the invisible, the universe is a dynamic and ever-changing tapestry in which all things are connected.

This dance is a celebration of unity, a reminder that we are part of a larger, harmonious whole. By embracing the seen and unseen worlds, we can begin to see the beauty in all things, to appreciate the interconnectedness of existence, and to live in harmony with the universe.

As we continue on our journey, let us carry with us the knowledge that we are not separate from the world, but an integral part of it. Let us embrace the infinite dance of existence, and let us find joy and meaning in the unity that lies at the heart of all things.

"In the grand tapestry of existence, every thread, seen and unseen, is woven into a single, harmonious whole. From the smallest particle to the vastness of the cosmos, the universe speaks a language of unity and connection, inviting us to bridge the worlds we know with those that lie beyond perception."

Summary

In *Spectrums Unseen*, we journey through a world hidden from our direct perception, exploring the dimensions, forces, and patterns that shape the universe in ways we are only beginning to understand.

Each chapter delves into a unique aspect of this invisible realm, from the dark matter that forms the cosmic web to the human microbiome that sustains our very lives. Along the way, we encounter the repeating fractals of nature, the power of magnetic fields, and the role of technology in extending our perception beyond biological limits.

Throughout this journey, we ponder questions of existence, consciousness, and the boundaries of reality. Are we truly alone in the universe, or are we part of a larger, multidimensional tapestry?

What hidden forces govern our world, and how might they reveal themselves to those who seek to understand them? As we explore these questions, we are reminded that there is more to the universe than meets the eye, and that our pursuit of knowledge will always lead us to new horizons.

By weaving together scientific inquiry, philosophical reflection, and a deep sense of wonder, *Spectrums Unseen* encourages readers to embrace the mystery of existence and to consider the vastness of reality beyond the boundaries of human perception. It is a celebration of the unknown, an invitation to explore the invisible dimensions that shape our lives, and a reminder that in every moment, we are surrounded by spectrums unseen.

Glossary

Antimatter: Matter composed of antiparticles, which have the same mass as particles of ordinary matter but opposite charges. When matter and antimatter collide, they annihilate each other, releasing energy.

Big Bang: The prevailing cosmological model that explains the early development of the universe. According to this model, the universe expanded from a very high-density and high-temperature state around 13.8 billion years ago.

Black Hole: A region of space with a gravitational pull so strong that nothing, not even light, can escape from it. Black holes are often formed when massive stars collapse under their own gravity.

Consciousness: The state of being aware of and able to think about one's surroundings, thoughts, and experiences. Some theories suggest that consciousness plays a role in shaping reality, especially at the quantum level.

Cosmic Microwave Background (CMB): The remnant radiation from the Big Bang, filling the universe. It is one of the oldest forms of light and provides critical insights into the early universe.

Dark Energy: A mysterious force that is driving the accelerated expansion of the universe. It is believed to make up about 68% of the universe's total energy.

Dark Matter: An unknown form of matter that does not emit or interact with electromagnetic radiation like ordinary matter. It makes up about 85% of the matter in the universe and is detected only through its gravitational effects.

Dimension: A measurable extent of a particular kind, such as length, breadth, depth, or time. In physics, the idea of multiple dimensions beyond the three spatial ones is often explored to explain complex phenomena like string theory.

Echolocation: A method used by animals such as bats and dolphins to locate objects by emitting sound waves and interpreting the echoes that return.

Electromagnetic Spectrum: The range of all types of electromagnetic radiation, from radio waves to gamma rays, including visible light. Only a small portion of the spectrum is visible to the human eye.

Fractals: Complex geometric shapes that exhibit self-similarity at different scales. Fractals are found in nature, such as in snowflakes, mountain ranges, and tree branches.

General Relativity: Albert Einstein's theory of gravitation, which describes gravity as a curvature of spacetime caused by mass and energy.

Gravitational Waves: Ripples in spacetime caused by accelerating massive objects like black holes and neutron stars. First directly detected in 2015, these waves provide new ways to observe cosmic events.

Higgs Boson: A fundamental particle associated with the Higgs field, which gives mass to other particles. Its discovery in 2012 confirmed a key part of the Standard Model of particle physics.

Multiverse: The hypothetical set of multiple universes, including our own, that may exist simultaneously. Some theories suggest that each universe could have different physical laws and dimensions.

Neutron Star: The dense remnants of a supernova explosion. Neutron stars are incredibly compact, with a mass greater than the Sun but only a few kilometres in diameter.

Quantum Mechanics: The branch of physics that deals with phenomena at very small scales, such as atoms and subatomic particles. Quantum mechanics challenges many classical notions of reality, especially with its implications for observation and uncertainty.

Relativity: A theory, particularly Einstein's general and special relativity, that explains how objects move and behave in space and time, especially at high speeds and in strong gravitational fields.

Simulation Hypothesis: The proposition that reality could be an artificial simulation, such as a computer-generated environment, created by advanced beings or civilizations.

Spacetime: The four-dimensional continuum consisting of three spatial dimensions and one time dimension, which are woven together to form the fabric of the universe in Einstein's theory of relativity.

String Theory: A theoretical framework in which the point-like particles of particle physics are replaced by one-dimensional objects known as strings. String theory suggests the existence of extra dimensions beyond the three spatial ones.

Time Dilation: A phenomenon in which time passes more slowly for an object moving close to the speed of light or in a strong gravitational field, as predicted by Einstein's theory of relativity.

Virtual Reality (VR): A simulated environment that can be similar to or completely different from the real world. VR is typically experienced through a computer-generated simulation that users can interact with.